Skiing Out of Your Mind

The Psychology of Peak Performance

Leonard A. Loudis, EdD
Denver, Colorado

W. Charles Lobitz, PhD
University of Colorado, Denver

Kenneth M. Singer, PhD
Keystone, Colorado

Leisure Press
A division of Human Kinetics Publishers, Inc.
Champaign, Illinois

Library of Congress Cataloging-in-Publication Data

Loudis, Leonard A.
    Skiing out of your mind.

    Bibliography: p.
    1. Skis and skiing—Psychological aspects. 2. Mind
and body. 3. Motivation (Psychology) 4. Performance.
I. Lobitz, W. Charles. II. Singer, Kenneth M.,
1934-   . III. Title.
GV854.9.P75L69   1986   796.93'01'9   85-18210
ISBN 0-88011-268-9

Editor: Peg Goyette
Production Director: Sara Chilton
Typesetters: Aurora Garcia and Angela Snyder
Text Layout: Gail Irwin
Book Design: Julie Szamocki
Printed by: Phillips Brothers
Cover Photo: Colorado Ski Country (Peter Runyon)
Back Cover Photo: Jean Eisenhour

ISBN: 0-88011-268-9
Copyright © 1986 by Leonard A. Loudis, W. Charles Lobitz, and
Kenneth M. Singer

Printed in the United States of America
10   9   8   7   6   5   4   3   2

Published by Leisure Press
A division of Human Kinetics Publishers, Inc.
Box 5076
Champaign, IL 61825-5076

UK Office:
Human Kinetics Publishers (UK) Ltd.
PO Box 18
Rawdon, Leeds LS19 6TG
England
(0532) 504211

Dedications

To Marcia, and to very special affiliates
#1, #1, and #1—Peter, Jon, and Laura.

L.A.L.

To the next generation of skiers—
Andrew, Peter, and Charlie Watts; Ogie,
Adam, and Ben Young; Kevin Carroll;
and Hilary and Heather Lobitz.

W.C.L.

To my friend Horace Ableman, super
skier; to my wife, Britta, super reader;
and especially to my daughter Arie,
super kid.

K.M.S.

Acknowledgments

We wish to thank all of our friends and students, who through their improved performance are evidence of the effectiveness of the *Skiing Out of Your Mind* approach.

A special note of thanks to Walter C. Lobitz, Jr., Marcia Goldin, Jane Brown, and Peg Goyette for their patient multiple readings of the manuscript and their thoughtful editorial comments.

Finally, for their inspiration, energy, and ski companionship we owe a special debt of gratitude to Horst Abraham, John Lobitz, Gretchen Lobitz, Gabrielle Hale-Blake, Frank Dumler, Pete Feistman, Boot Gordon, Ellie Manzi, Julia Tuschman, Barbara McAllister, and Gary Gilbert. Thank you all!

L.A.L.
W.C.L.
K.M.S.
Denver, 1985

C O N T E N T S

Foreword

by Horst Abraham*

What is the mind? Science is answering this age-old question only very slowly. Ever since Roger Sperry of the California Institute of Technology received a Nobel prize for his pioneering in brain research, a new fraternity has been formed by professionals and lay persons in order to put new research findings to work. Today our society is focusing its attention on the exploration of the macrospace of the universe. But I believe the true catalyst for future development will be our growing understanding of the human state and the microspace of the brain. It is the operational center within each of us that regulates movement, health, emotions, perceptions, and creativity. Though insignificant in size, it is the most sophisticated computer in existence and holds the key to yet unknown dimensions of human capacities.

We are just now discovering how limitless the mind's powers really are. On the average, we use only a small fraction of our physical or intellectual potential. Even world-class athletes have not yet reached their full potential, although they continue to set new records each year. Athletes attribute at least 50% of their winning edge to mental fitness. Alternative teaching methods expand long-term memory by as much as 60%. We can learn to read 800 to 1,000 words per minute.

---

*Horst is the manager of Training and Development with the Vail/Beaver Creek Ski School; the Director of Research and Development for the Professional Ski Instructors of America; the author of Skiing Right (New York: Harper & Row); the co-author of Skiing for Women; and an extensively published freelance writer.

We can learn foreign languages in 20 half-days. Medical wonders are achieved with placebo and belief therapy. Voodoo and stigmata suddenly are explainable.

As we deal with such dimensions, we must understand that we are not just dealing with fantasies but are really opening up new possibilities. Skiing offers us a special opportunity for practicing physical and mental skills. Skiing bombards a person almost simultaneously with tension and relaxation, with terror and exhilaration, with clarity and illusion, with exhaustion and recuperation. How often do we become frustrated on those days when we seem unable to perform even well known skills? How seldom, by contrast, do we experience the exhilaration of being able to perform the most difficult tasks with ease, grace, rhythm, and unwavering confidence? If only we could bring out our best performance more predictably and more often!

This book shows us exactly that: how to perform at peak performance levels by choice, not chance. Authors Loudis and Lobitz are clinical psychologists with considerable experience in applying psychology to sport. Len Loudis is an expert skier who has honed his skill by systematically applying the principles he now writes about. Chuck Lobitz, an outstanding skier for years, was a top racer in college and a successful coach before becoming a psychologist and applying these principles to skiing. Ken Singer is a teacher at the Vail Ski School—a creative teacher at a ski school that has the highest standards for its instructors. Singer has also conducted many workshops on stress and on mind/body skiing.

Together these three authors present their formula for success. In a comprehensive and understandable form, they identify the elements of consistency in performance and offer proven strategies for programming oneself to succeed. They share a basic value—that the reader should *learn to learn*. The transferability of such knowledge and skills is unlimited. The authors identify self-generated barriers to learning and performance in the form of self-talk and self-image. They offer viable alternatives to self-criticism and negative self-talk. Most of us are limited by an array of bad habits. Many of us would perhaps resign ourselves to the fate of living with our undesirable habits, but Loudis, Lobitz, and Singer tell us we can change all that. And they show us how.

This book makes good use of examples, metaphors, and anecdotes to explain and reinforce the authors' points. It is highly readable and infinitely practical, and few are the readers who will not become better learners and better skiers. This book's inescapable influence lies in the way it combines sound scientific concepts with practical strategies. I rank it as one of the best available on skiing. Better yet, because it is based on psychological principles that apply not only to skiing but also to living, the reader can't help but gain from applying the strategies offered herein.

Preface

*All our power lies in both mind and body;
we employ the mind to rule, the body to
serve.*

Gaius Sallustius Crispus, from *The War With Catiline*
(c. 40 B.C.)

For over 2,000 years, we have been aware of the mind's importance in controlling the performance of the body. And for probably just as long, we have known that the two do not always function in concert. Despite our awareness of these ancient wisdoms, only recently has anyone tried to utilize this knowledge to enhance sport performance. About 10 years ago the Soviets and East Germans began systematically applying psychological principles to their athletic training programs. Their combined win of 89 gold, 66 silver, and 60 bronze medals in the 1976 Olympic Games electrified the sports world, and American coaches, athletes, and psychologists began to concentrate on the mental aspect of sports.

The most popular focus in those early days was the "inner game" approach, pioneered by Tim Gallwey, a tennis player who applied Eastern philosophy and meditation to quieting the mind. This first step emphasized removing mental distraction from physical performance. At the same time, psychologists such as Dr. Richard Suinn and Dr. Michael Mahoney were applying cognitive and behavioral psychology techniques in their work with U.S. athletes. In Colorado, we were excited by the potential of using both of these approaches to enhance skiing performance. The combination of cognitive/behavioral psychology and Eastern/meditative philosophy promised a power that was greater than the sum of its parts.

We began applying this combination to skiing in the mid-1970s, and in 1977 we wrote *Skiing From the Head Down: A Psychological Approach* (J.B. Lippincott). Over the next 7 years, we conducted workshops for instructors, coaches, racers, and recreational skiers in the application of psychology to skiing. We were joined by Dr. Ken Singer, an instructor with the Vail Ski School, who utilized our approaches with his students and who refined and expanded the techniques to their present level of effectiveness.

As our own experience has grown since 1977, so has the field of sport psychology. *Skiing Out of Your Mind: The Psychology of Peak Performance* reflects this growth. We build upon the solid foundation of the first book with a great deal of new material. The chapter on active awareness, an important starting point for the application of mental skills in skiing, now includes a self-test on your present use of psychological tactics, as well as detailed instruction on how to develop your kinesthetic awareness (your sense of your body in space and motion). The chapter on relaxation now includes material on the powerful technique of negative practice, and the chapter on metaphors is almost entirely new. In addition to many new examples throughout the book, other material has been changed extensively.

We address the needs of advanced skiers, professionals, and competitors in a total of six entirely new chapters and appendices. The new chapters are mental imagery, concentration, and belief and confidence; the three appendices offer further thoughts on the practical application of mental skills techniques for ski instructors and competitors.

The basic process of applying psychology to your skiing remains unchanged, however: It is a process of experiencing with your body plus thinking with your mind, and of inner awareness plus outer awareness. It works for beginners and experts alike. Just as it has helped skiers in our workshops and classes to maximize their performance, we expect it will help you to reach your peak level of skiing.

But skiing is not magic. Neither is *Skiing Out of Your Mind.* Do not expect that merely by reading this book you will be able to magically achieve a peak in your skiing performance. The mind and the body do not work that way. They work according to a set of well established psychological principles.

You were not born knowing how to ski. Almost everything about your skiing, the performance of your mind as well as your body, has been learned. This is why you may have developed some bad habits in skiing. We all *learned* them in accordance with well established psychological principles, including our response to an innate instinct for self-preservation and balance. Furthermore, not only did we learn all our bad physical habits, we also learned all our bad mental habits: our fear reactions, our self-criticism, our poor concentration. Does that sound depressing? Don't despair. The good news is that the psychological mechanisms so effective in causing our problems in the first place are equally powerful in helping us to get rid of them. In addition, they are the same mechanisms by which we acquire positive habits, the ones that lead to our confidence, our joy, and our peak performances.

Skiing takes work. So does *Skiing Out of Your Mind*. The application of psychological principles to achieve peak performance requires active, dedicated participation on your part—and disciplined practice with the mental work—just as improvement in your ski technique requires disciplined practice with the physical work. This is not to say that working on your skiing, mentally or physically, cannot be fun. After all, you ski because you love it. And as Dr. Scott Peck said about love in *The Road Less Travelled*, "Love is discipline." Truly working on your skiing takes discipline; it is a labor of love, complete with pains and joys. Like loving, mental work can be a powerful but intangible experience. And, like loving, if you do not find skiing to be much fun, you probably will not spend much time out there doing it anyway.

To put it another way, *Skiing Out of Your Mind* does not mean skiing *without* your mind. It means skiing *from out of* your mind. Your mind is the base from which to build your peak performance. It is the foundation for your learning and your improvement. We are confident that if you approach the material in this book with that commitment and dedication, you will experience those physical and emotional peaks.

Best wishes and many happy turns!

L.A.L.
W.C.L.
K.M.S.

CHAPTER 1

Psychology and Skiing

You get up one morning and look out on a clear winter landscape. Ten inches of new snow! You cover the distance from bed to breakfast to mountain in three leaps and 20 minutes. The chairlift is just opening as you hit the lift line. You have to keep from diving out of the chair before you reach the top, the snow is so inviting. Blasting off down a wide-open field of untouched powder, you feel the cold, dry crystals billow around you. Each turn sends a frosty white wave over your head. You are soaring above the earth; you are diving to the bottom of the sea. Euphoria fills your heart, rings in your ears, teases your palate, tickles your nose. Fantastic! When you get to the bottom, you turn to watch another skier dance down the field of powder, cutting tracks parallel to yours. You exchange grins of ecstasy at the end of the run, sharing your joy.

Something about skiing can create what psychologists call "a peak experience." A good day of skiing satisfies our need for grace, beauty, motion, mastery, danger, and acceleration. Those satisfactions keep bringing us back to the mountains day after day, season after season, and dollar after dollar.

Unfortunately, skiing is not always a peak experience. When you are having a bad day, your only peak experiences are spelled p-i-q-u-e, at best. There is no grace, beauty, or mastery when you are angry, frightened, cold, wet, or aching. Yet, that is also a part of skiing. Our experience with psychology includes both the *peak* experiences and the *pique* experiences. The skiers we know would like to have more of the former and less of the latter. This book is written to help them, and you, accomplish just that.

Mindful or Mindless?

This book is also written for the skier who believes that having a brain is an asset in skiing. However, most skiers do not know how to use their brains to help their skiing. Generally there are two groups of such skiers, both of them frustrated: the people whose minds get in the way of their skiing, and the people who don't use their minds at all. Both types want to improve but don't know how to take advantage of their brains to get the most improvement and enjoyment from the sport. Just as you and your body can learn ski technique, so can you and your mind discover how to increase your peak experiences on skis.

What is skiing like for the people whose minds get in their way? They approach a day of skiing by *thinking* themselves into a state of near-paralysis. Before they get to the slope they worry about the weather, the conditions, and the lift lines. They contemplate taking the day off, or just buying a half-day ticket, or skiing the easier slopes. Clearly imprinted in their minds may be the falls they took on their last run the day before, the pain of their new boots, or the size of the moguls on their favorite hills. Then, just as they are about ready to spend the day in front of the TV set, they remember all the money spent on new equipment, lift tickets, and lessons, and decide to swallow their fear and ski anyway. On the way up the lift, they watch the skiers below sliding on the ice, careening off the bumps, or disappearing head first into the powder. By now the fear that they swallowed is stuck in the middle of their throats. Of course, some skiers on the slope below are skiing well and enjoying themselves, but the skiers whose minds get in the way just envy them with a sigh: "If only I could ski like that." By the time they get off the lift and start their first run, they are so stiff that they are thrown by the first bump and fall in a heap of embarrassment reminiscent of their first days on skis. Then, as if their *fear* were not enough, they get *angry* at themselves for skiing like that. This is the "psyched out" approach to skiing.

What about the skiers who don't use their minds at all? Although they are generally fewer in number, some of you may be among them. They begin the day—in the words of a friend of ours—"by sending their brains out for a beer." Their brains never return. They are largely unconscious of conditions or terrain and head immediately for the expert runs. They pursue those black diamond trail signs marked "most difficult"as though they were veins of gold ore. Without even adjusting their goggles they blast off the first set of bumps they can find, do an involuntary half-gainer in a full-layout position and, if they're lucky, eject from both bindings. They can usually be spotted after the first run, looking as though they've just emerged from a blizzard when there has not been any fresh powder in a week. They are also the skiers who cannot understand why, after all the lessons they've had and all the skiing they've done (they are usually the last ones off the mountain each day), they have not improved in years. We call this the "Look, Ma, No Brains" approach.

We realize that both types are extremes, but we want to make an important point: There is a part of them in all of us. They represent how *not* to use our minds to get the most out of our skiing. This is not limited to beginning or intermediate skiers. Experts and competitors psych themselves out of good skiing as well. It is not easy to know how to use your mind to get the most out of your skiing. You have put a lot of time, energy, and money into your skiing. You may have gotten yourself into reasonable physical shape from systematic, off-the-snow conditioning, purchased good equipment and clothing, and taken lessons from a qualified instructor. You may even have read some good books on ski technique. In short, you have devoted a lot of attention to how to ski with your body. Unfortunately, you have not devoted much attention to how to ski with your mind. This is not surprising, and you are certainly not to blame. Nobody has told you that you should use your mind when skiing, nor has anyone told you how to use your mind. When we say "told you how," we are referring to certain specific, highly useful psychological tactics for skiing that can be taught just as you have been taught to set your edges or flex your legs. And when we say "use your mind," we also mean knowing how to get it out of the way when necessary.

Until a few years ago, if you wanted to learn about skiing you went to a ski school, and if you wanted to learn about psychology you registered for a psychology course. Yet if you watched either the 1984 Winter or Summer Olympics, you know how much attention athletes and their coaches are devoting to sport psychology. The psychological principles that help the best athletes in the world can also help you.

This book is written for all skiers. The techniques are useful at any level, and improvement can be dramatic at all levels. We have written it out of our experience as skiers, ski instructors, and psychologists. What, you ask, do psychologists know about skiing? In general, probably no more than any other group. What we do know is something about how people learn and how they change their behavior. Since to learn skiing you must change how you behave, the principles of psychology are relevant to the sport, probably more relevant than you ever imagined. As psychologists, we also know something about how people think. "But what does thinking have to do with skiing?" you may ask. "The last time I tried to think my way into a turn, my skis went straight into the woods." True enough. You cannot intellectualize your movements, or your mistakes. If all you do is think about skiing, you may as well leave your body at home in an easy chair. We are not talking about using your mind as a substitute for your body. We are talking about knowing *when* and *how* to use your mind to supplement your body. They work best in harmony.

Skiing is a Risk Sport

Psychology is important to all recreational sports, but there is one factor that makes skiing more difficult to learn than golf, tennis, or running. *Skiing is a risk sport.* This is impressed upon you all too often when you see an unfortunate fellow skier lashed tightly to a sled, wincing as he or she takes the bumpy ride down to the X-ray table. Can you recall what went through your mind the last time you saw this happen? Do you remember how your body felt the last time you stood at the top of a steep, bumpy slope? If you wondered how you would get down in one piece, then your heart raced, your breath quickened, your mouth felt dry, and your legs felt weak. Your body was experiencing all the physiological signs of fear. If you were aware of your mind, you probably noticed that it was also showing signs of fear, with thoughts like "I can't make it. Why did I take this trail? I'm not a good skier, anyway. Isn't there a cutoff around this pitch?" There are two main difficulties with fear, even in its mild form, called anxiety. One is that it is unpleasant to experience. You know that. The other is that it interferes with *learning*. We know that.

Risk and Fear

Isn't risk a part of skiing? You may get a lot of kicks out of the risk in skiing. You love to go fast, to take chances. Encountering and overcoming danger is exhilarating. Skiing wouldn't be such a peak experience if there were not some risk involved. The problem for most of us is that at some point in our skiing we become *afraid*. And when we do, our skiing falls apart. There is an important difference between risk and fear. *The risk is out there; the fear is inside you.* The only way to avoid the risk is to stop skiing. But if you learn to manage the fear, you will be left with joy and exhilaration. This little equation is worth remembering:

Risk minus fear = peak experience

We want to help you manage the fear. The risk is up to you. To be fair, we recognize that fear is not the only emotion that can interfere with the joy of skiing. Anger can also ruin a good day. This is especially true for advanced skiers and racers. If you fit into this category, you know that even though you have learned to love the risk in skiing, you are still susceptible to feelings of impatience and frustration when you are not skiing up to your potential. For you the equation should read: Risk minus anger = peak experience.

Peak Performance and Arousal

For all skiers, from novices to racers, peak experience is a function of *peak performance*. We enjoy the sport most when we are performing at our maximum level. So how do we reach this maximum, this peak level? The answer is what this book is all about. And the answer begins with one of the basic laws of psychology: *Performance is a function of arousal.* However, the relationship is not linear. As you can see from the performance/arousal curve in Figure 1, it is only half true that the more aroused we are, the better we perform. We all know that a certain amount of arousal or excitement will enhance our performance. That is the first half of the truth. The second half is that *after a certain point, high levels of arousal actually inhibit our performance.* A prime example of this is the ski racer who does well in training but often "chokes" in competition. It is not that he or she has lost any ability on race day. Rather, it is that the racer has become *too* aroused to perform at a peak level. The curve in Figure 1 depicts this relationship. At the top of this performance/arousal curve, not only are you performing at your highest level but also you are likely to be entertaining yourself with a peak experience.

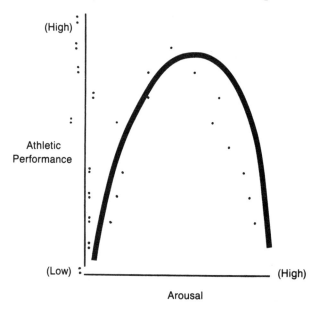

Figure 1 — The performance/arousal curve.

From the curve, you can see that to reach your highest level of performance you must learn to control your level of arousal, keeping it as near the optimum level as possible. If you are under-aroused, you can enhance your performance (and your peak experience) by becoming psyched-up. On the other hand, if you are psyched-out, you will need to decrease your arousal in order to perform at your peak. This ability to center your arousal is crucial to peak performance. We will be covering it thoroughly in upcoming chapters.

Peak Performance and Learning

What a lousy day. Boots hurt. Goggles fogged up again. Gotta stop. Can't see anything, anyway. How do you ski on a day like this? The snow is terrible. Too heavy. Why am I having such a hard time on this hill? Look at that idiot. I can't believe anyone like that can ski so effortlessly. Gotta be crazy. Why can't I do that? Why am I doing what I'm doing?

Does this conversation with yourself sound familiar? You are trying desperately to learn to ski well but the skill is eluding you. You get frustrated. Perhaps you yell at yourself. Maybe you swear. You let loose your finest expletives, slamming your pole against a mogul that just coolly sits there. Or maybe you just cry quietly after a fall. At the same time, is your friend, coach, spouse, or child exhorting you to get up?

Good News and Bad News

First, the bad news: From the psychological standpoint, *you have learned to ski like that.* "Wait!" you object. "I don't want to ski (or think) like that. I don't like being angry at myself. I don't like feeling frustrated or afraid. I don't like any part of it. It's not my fault. That's just the way I am!"

All you say is true, of course. You do not want to ski like that. And you certainly do not want to act like that when you ski. But you were not born that way. Obviously, you were not born a skier at all. Just as you have learned everything you know about good skiing, you have also learned everything you know about faulty skiing—faulty mind habits as well as faulty body habits. Knowing that you have learned it is the best insight you could have right now, because this takes the mystery out of getting to be a good skier or better competitor. It also helps explain why, with identical technique lessons, some people progress to become good skiers while others don't progress at all.

Now the good news: As psychologists, we know that many of your problems are mind problems and can be relearned. Relearning simply applies the same principles that were involved when you developed those problems in the first place. However, instead of letting them occur arbitrarily in the same way you acquired your faulty habits, you can plan the psychological process ahead of time and use it to your advantage, systematically, to achieve your goals.

Relearning is a conscious process. Many people have trouble accepting the idea that they learned their habits, including the physical techniques for the body and the psychological habits of the mind. "How could I have learned to do all those self-destructive things?" one of our skier friends once asked. "I didn't study bad habits, you know." That's just it. Most skiers are not actively aware of their learning, but it goes on anyway, even without their awareness. As research in psychology has shown, we learn in ways much more subtle than we ever imagined. In our experience, many skiers do not begin to relearn until they become *aware*. That is why the relearning in this book is a *conscious* process. In order to *Ski Out of Your Mind*, you first need to wake your mind up.

What do we mean by relearning? We have found that skiers commonly have in mind one or more of three general goals when they say they want to learn to ski and/or compete better. There is a great deal of overlap among the goals, but this breakdown is useful nonetheless. (1) You may want to *increase* certain skiing skills. (2) You may want to *decrease* or eliminate some faulty habits you have picked up. (3) You may want to change some strong emotional feelings or fears you have.

Here are some common examples of the first goal, prefaced by "I wish..."

- that I could just be a little more aggressive.
- that I could ski faster.
- that I could flex my knees more.

- that I could concentrate better in the gates.
- that I could let my skis flow in the bumps.

The second goal is prefaced by a futile "If only..."

- I could stop stiffening my downhill leg.
- I crossed my tips less often.
- I stopped yelling at myself (or my friends).

Closely interacting with the first two goals are these emotional changes you would like to make:

- Why am I so afraid of a slightly steeper hill?
- I don't like sharp moguls on narrow trails.
- I wish I didn't feel so frightened of falling.
- I can't stand snowy days and flat light.

Yet all of the "I wishes" and "if onlys" in the world are not going to help you ski better. If you recognize yourself in any of the examples, you are probably aware of this truth and would rather not be reminded of it! But if you really want to improve, you will need to work with your mind as well as your body, with your thoughts and feelings as well as your skiing skills.

Right Brain, Left Brain: The Metaphor

Thus far we have been talking about achieving a balance between mind and body. There is another kind of equilibrium that we want to address: brain balance. You know that your brain has two structurally similar halves, the right and left brain (technically, the right and left cerebral hemispheres). In most ways the two halves of the brain have similar functions. However, both folklore and some early scientific evidence suggested that each side of the brain is responsible for different processes.

In this view, those separate processes correspond to the two sides of human consciousness. Dr. Robert Ornstein, a psychologist, has investigated the dual nature of human consciousness from biological, psychological, and cultural perspectives. In *The Psychology of Consciousness*, he points out that the Hopi Indians of the Southwest draw a right-left distinction between intellectual and intuitive activity, attributing the function of writing to one side and the function of music to the other. The Eastern religious philosophy of Vedanta distinguishes between buddhi (intellect) and manas (mind). And the Chinese yin-yang symbol expresses the bipolar and complementary aspects of human consciousness. One side represents spirit and time, the other represents nature and space.

This concept of duality in our consciousness is supported by some medical research into the different functions of the right and left sides of the brain. The left side seems more important for intellectual, analytic work, whereas the right side seems more important for holistic, intuitive work. The former is associated with logic, reasoning, and linear thinking. The latter is associated with spatial relations, gestalts, and experiencing. Furthermore, research suggests that the two sides of the brain seem to complement each other in that we use one or the other mode of consciousness, but not both, at any one time (although the hemispheres do communicate with one another). This means that if you were concentrating on solving a verbal, intellectual problem, you would have more difficulty balancing on a rail fence (or skis) than if you were not. And vice versa. Dr. R.W. Sperry, in a scientific article, suggested that each hemisphere has its own separate and private sensations, its own perceptions and concepts and impulses to act, with related volitional, cognitive, and learning experiences.

More recent neuropsychological research suggests that the functions of each side of the brain are not so simply divided, however, and that there is a great deal of overlap and integration between the two hemispheres. However, we still find this model to be a useful metaphor from which to operate. We will use this metaphor to help you think about your awareness in different modes.

So what does this have to do with skiing? Given that the right brain is more spatial and experiential and the left brain is more logical and intellectual, what happens to your skiing if you try to *think* about every motion? If you are using your left brain (linear thinking) while engaging in a physical, holistic experience such as skiing, you are likely to find that you have left your coordination at the starting gate. The effect on your skiing of too much thinking is characteristic of the first type of frustrated skiers we identified at the beginning of this chapter. They thought their way into a state of near-paralysis. On the other hand, or more accurately, on the other side of the brain, a total reliance on *experiencing* without any thought at all can be equally devastating. Skiers who "send their brains out for a beer" end up cold, wet, aching, and unimproved. However, a combination of left- and right-brain activity can lead to some pretty gratifying experiences on skis, like the following for one of us:

During my years of competitive racing, I had the opportunity to compete in the North American Alpine Championships, held that year at Cannon Mtn. in New Hampshire. On the day of the slalom, I was excited but a little intimidated because many of the other racers had more natural ability and more experience than I. When I saw the course, I wondered if I wouldn't be a lot happier sitting in the lodge, sipping a hot buttered rum! The hill was extremely steep and icy, and the turns were so tight that the course seemed designed for midgets. I felt myself start to get tense. "This is ridiculous," I thought. "I'm doing this because I enjoy it, so why am I feeling so nervous? Maybe I think the competition is over my head. Sure, there are some hot skiers here, but that's what competition is about. My nervousness is a signal to me that this race is exciting. I just need to use that excitement to do my best. If I didn't belong in this race, I wouldn't have been invited anyway." (Without realizing it, I was using positive self-talk to relax and control my anticipatory anxiety.)

I turned my attention to learning the course. Every section demanded concentration, rhythm, and caution. "Don't go for broke on this one. The whole course is a killer. Smoothness is the key. The speed will take care of itself," I told myself. I was really thinking about this one, planning my attack against a course that could trip me up at every turn.

I loosened up by making tight, smooth turns above the start. I felt good. I had planned my strategy in my mind. Now it was time to start experiencing the rhythm I wanted. I did not know it at the time, but I was now shifting my activity from my left to my right brain. When I got in the starting gate, I wasn't thinking at all. My concentration was on a rhythmical experience. When I pushed out of the gate, it was smoothness all the way down. I felt great. And I didn't think again until after the finish.

The other racers didn't fare so well. Skier after skier blasted off the course or became entangled in a forest of poles. No strategy, no rhythm. After the first run, I was in sixth place, 1.5 seconds out of first.

I studied the second course. It was like the first—steep, tight, treacherous. "Same story, same strategy. Go for rhythm. Make round turns. The speed will take care of it- self," I thought. I crossed the finish line feeling like a ballet dancer. It was fantastic. When the race was over, I was in fourth place and only 0.8 of a second behind the winner. No medals, but a lot of satisfaction. I had beaten a lot of better skiers, I had beaten the course, but I had not beaten myself.

There is a time and a place for linear thinking in skiing. There is also a time and a place for nonlinear thinking. We think both are necessary for *Skiing Out of Your Mind*. We have also experienced the need for both. We do not wish to emphasize one side of the brain over the other. We do not intend to perform psychosurgery on one half of your mind by suggesting that you tune out your thoughts or disconnect your experiences. Your brain works best if it is left intact. Our pur- pose is to help you integrate your thoughts, feelings, and ex- periences so you can use your mind to help your body.

Coming Attractions

The next two chapters define and illustrate the common mind problems that skiers, including ourselves, are prone to. We will discuss the psychological basis for these problems, with an emphasis on taking the mystery out of how you learn both good and bad habits. We will separate the relearning process into its elements. This breakdown is artificial, but we believe it is necessary to enable you to specify your own prob- lem areas, understand why they are maintained, and design an efficient way to change them. Your clear understanding of your problems and how you acquired them is powerful information to have when you choose to begin the change process. You will recognize yourself (perhaps painfully!) in parts of these chapters. Of course, since individuals differ in their psychological make-up, some examples may not apply to you.

Chapter 4 initiates you into the active part of working with your skiing psychology. It describes the process of defining where you are and where you want to go. The remaining chapters employ the psychological techniques of *Skiing Out of Your Mind*. They are not just a collection of ideas or hunches. Some have evolved from research by a great many psychologists; other tactics come from our work on the ski slopes and our clinical practices. They represent the merging of our experience as skiers and our knowledge as psychologists.

In the end, we take your skiing as a total experience, without obsessing or over-analyzing, and especially without intellectualizing. We want you to let go, to feel, to be aware of your relationship with the mountain in space and time. We view skiing as a flowing process. This is right-brain stuff. It all fits together as an entire experience, a gestalt, an integration of your body and mind that, when working right, seems almost spiritual in its beauty and grace. We feel it is an intense individual challenge, a communication between a lone skier and a mountain that is itself as complex in variety as you are in your feelings and thoughts and ways of skiing.

DANGER

CHAPTER 2

It's Frightening What Fear Does to Your Skiing

Watch young children rocketing joyfully through the bumps. They are as close to being natural skiers as anybody can be. Even when falling down, they display little of the awkwardness and hesitancy that are characteristic of adult skiers. Why do children seem so much looser than adults? First, as we grow, our bodies become less resilient, making it more unpleasant for us to fall. When children do a half-gainer into a snowbank at 10:30 in the morning, they do not feel crippled for the next couple of runs. Nor do they immediately think they ought to go in for lunch or retire to the hot tub. They do get discouraged, but their discouragement usually comes as a result of being cold, bored, or lonely. They are not discouraged about their skiing as often as adults are.

Second, adults develop what is euphemistically termed "discretion," but more accurately called "fear." When you "risk" yourself, when you put yourself into the position of losing your balance and maybe falling, many involuntary systems within your body take over. This is not an idea or an opinion, it is a neurological fact. Your nervous system is wired up that way. What it boils down to, of course, is that humans are "wired" for self-preservation. Many of the ski positions in which you find yourself are unstable. It is as true when you are learning to do your first parallel turn as it is when you are skiing your first deep powder. When you are unstable, the vestibular system in your inner ear detects that you are losing your balance. You respond involuntarily. Reflexively you experience a stiffening of your muscles. At the same time you most likely get a rush. Your heart speeds up, you breathe faster, adrenalin is released into your bloodstream, and blood is shifted to your major muscle systems. In other words, you experience an emergency reaction.

The Psychology of Fear

As humans, we do not just absorb sensory stimuli; we actively process our experiences, responding to the world and our bodies as we perceive them to be. Each of us, of course, sees the world differently. One skier may perceive the rush experienced when almost falling as just that and no more. This person may say, "Wow! I almost fell; I could feel my body beginning to stiffen.... Just relax. Get under control again." If this is you, you are the exception. Most skiers don't react with this kind of equanimity despite the fact that this interpretation is the accurate one. You did almost fall. What you experienced was the rush that normally accompanies loss of balance, and it can be perceived as such without imagining potential catastrophes. As you will see shortly, those few skiers who interpret experiences this way are ahead of the game.

The more typical response is something like, "Whew, that was close. Could have been a bad fall. Might have gotten hurt. Got to be more careful." This second reaction is the one that gets in the way. You have rehearsed in your mind how dangerously close you came to falling, how bad the fall could have been (or actually was). You have in fact *increased* the fear and apprehension. You have increased the probability of being tense. And you have certainly increased the likelihood that the feeling will occur again the next time you are in a similar situation, maybe only 30 feet farther down the mountain.

Not only is this second reaction the more common one but, based upon the way people have learned to respond to threatening situations, it may well be the normal one. That is why it is so inefficient for your body to teach itself to ski. As far as your body knows, tensing up is the normal neurological response to being unstable. As happens with all of us, your body and your mind get all mixed together. On or off skis, your body may do the same thing as the next person's. But your mind is different. In this example, your body has reacted naturally and reflexively to a loss of equilibrium. Your mind said, "Close call! I've got to be careful." Result: Your mind has plugged in a memory that losing your equilibrium equals being afraid. The next time you almost fall, you reexperience the fearful thought and you become more tense and more cautious. In a short time you become a skier of the utmost discretion.

Two crucial points about skiing psychology need to be made here:

1. If your mind says that the reflexive stiffening of your muscles (the normal response, remember) signaled a close call (danger), then your mind has gotten in the way of doing what you wanted your body to do. That is why you so frequently say to yourself, "Now why can't I do that? I *know* what I'm doing wrong. I just can't do it right!"
2. You have now set yourself up for a terribly self-defeating conclusion: "If I know what I'm doing wrong and still can't do it right, I'm never going to learn how. I'm just no good. I might as well quit."

These two ways of thinking are major reasons for slow improvement in your skiing. Look for a moment at how you got there. Based upon your evidence, you have made the logical conclusion. But based upon the real facts, you have not reached the correct conclusion. Your evidence was that you could see what others were doing that you were not. Since you found you could not just let your body do what it should, you concluded that something must be wrong—namely, you. Then you blamed yourself and lost hope.

However, the real facts are that you have ignored what fear has done to your skiing. Review the critical points. The only natural thing about learning to ski is the reflexive (automatic) response humans have to a loss of balance. The response is an emergency tensing of the muscles, for example stiffening of the downhill leg, leaning into the hill, tension of the musculature of your torso. As if that were not enough, you have responded with the predictable psychological fear reaction. This response was a *natural* one. Finally, you have taken a solid step toward psyching yourself out.

Emotional Learning

Thus far we have been discussing what is called "emotional learning." Your reflexive responses and most of your skiing feelings, like fear, are the result of this type of learning. Here is how it works: You experience the tensing that occurs when you have the emergency reaction. The reflexive reaction has occurred under a certain ski condition. It may be a sharp mogul for some of you, or heavy snow, icy runs, or gaining too much speed for others. The point is that it has occurred in conjunction with a certain stimulus, that is, a certain skiing condition.

Let's say the stimulus is a short series of sharp moguls. In psychological terms, the emergency reaction has been paired with that skiing condition because they occurred at the same time. You reflexively tensed up those muscles on the moguls. After several pairings of your reflexive emergency reaction with that stimulus, the sharp moguls will come to cause the tenseness *even without your losing your balance*. Thus, when you have had frightening experiences with certain snow conditions or types of runs, those conditions or runs will cause you to feel tense even before you get to them. All you have to do is *see* the moguls. What was a normal emergency reaction has now become a learned psychological response. Furthermore, conditions only moderately similar can also produce feelings of apprehension. And, as if that were not enough, simply *imagining* the situations can cause tension.

Consider for a moment the implications of this kind of emotional learning. Here you are, about to take a run. You make your first turns. Just ahead is one of those stimuli that have become capable of causing you apprehension, for example that series of moguls. You see them coming. You tense up and hit the first mogul stiffly instead of flexibly absorbing it. Whether you realize it or not, you have *learned* to do the exact opposite of what good mogul technique requires.

Thus, the fear-cues you have learned, which are different for all of us, have become a real problem: (1) They involuntarily caused your muscles to tense, and (2) they caused your mind to tense. When your mind is tense, you fail to think realistically and you lose concentration. You tend to think about potential catastrophes and ignore your body, your skis, and the terrain. And all of it was learned in a most normal and predictable way.

Operant Learning

Emotional learning has to do with reflexive responses and feelings about skiing, whereas operant learning has to do with skiing behaviors. Skiing obviously involves a series of voluntary physical behaviors. Setting your edges, bending your knees, and unweighting are all examples. You do them intentionally.

Operant learning, the learning of these voluntary behaviors, is largely dependent upon what kind of payoff you get for skiing the way you do. Does skiing that way look better? Does it give you a feeling of balance and grace? Such payoffs can be positive benefits. The thrill of a good powder run, a compliment from your friends, the sensation of setting your edges and beautifully carving a turn—all of these are positive. You will likely try to repeat these skiing behaviors on the next run because they have worked for you. You felt good. Like many other skiers, you probably have never taken the time to analyze how you acquired your good habits. It should now be easy to see how the positive result of a particular skiing behavior would tend to keep you skiing that way. You have received a genuine payoff for doing it, for example that compliment, that good feeling, or that sense of balance and grace.

Of more concern here, though, is the subtle way that fear influences your ski habits, in other words, how fear influences operant learning. Why do you keep avoiding that steeper slope or that field of moguls? Why do you persist in leaning too far into the hill? What possible payoff can there be for persisting with the stiff downhill leg when you know it is not right? The answer is basic to ski psychology; it has to do with the unfortunate but persistent effects of fear. It is based upon the same principles as those applied to good skiing habits and it also has to do with payoffs. Whenever your behavior helps you avoid or escape something fearful or unpleasant, that behavior is reinforced and becomes a stronger habit. In other words, the fact that you avoided discomfort is the payoff for the behavior. Anxiety and fear, even embarrassment and humiliation, are like that. If there is something you can voluntarily do to *decrease* your discomfort, aren't you likely to go ahead and voluntarily do it? After all, who likes to be uncomfortable?

It may make excellent sense, but it certainly does not make excellent skiing! Some examples of voluntarily avoiding discomfort are the following:

- Staying on the easier hills most of the day; thus you avoid the apprehension that accompanies the moguls, steep slopes, or whatever situation makes you tense up.
- Always stopping to your right (or left), thus avoiding uncomfortable feelings of instability when stopping the other way.
- Not doing a kick turn on steep terrain; instead, you probably plant your poles way below you and awkwardly step around. By doing this you avoid the fall you anticipated if you had kick-turned.
- Not skiing under the lift even though it may have the best snow; this way, you avoid the imagined humiliation you'd suffer if you should fall in front of others.
- Traversing across that heavily moguled hill, arms flailing, each bump throwing you further off balance; because you successfully avoid falling while doing this, you do not take the risk of linking your turns.
- Rotating your shoulders back into the hill in response to your feelings of instability.

We have come to another critical point on how your psychology influences your skiing. Notice that in each example the fear, uneasiness, and embarrassment you are avoiding are your own feelings. You carry the payoffs around in your mind every time you ski! Their influence on your skiing habits cannot be overestimated. In each case, the actions you have taught yourself are exactly opposite to what you should have done. Notice, too, that you are avoiding something that has been the result of earlier emotional learning. *The major reason that bad habits are so persistent is that you carry the payoffs with you in your mind!*

Stop for a moment here. If it is not clear how emotional learning (your feelings) influences your operant learning (your voluntary behaviors), go back and reread the examples. Then make up some of your own. What is the first bad habit that comes to mind? Define it. What do you see as the payoff for doing it? Does it decrease or avoid apprehension, or feelings of loss of balance? To work on your skiing psychology, you need to understand how your psychology works on your skiing. Thinking up your own examples is one of the best ways to do that.

Bad Habits Seem Forever

It may seem to you that the bad habits should just go away. In fact they are terribly frustrating, make you angry with yourself, and lead you unfailingly back to the old self-defeating syndrome. From a psychological standpoint there are two interrelated reasons for this resistance:

1. The payoffs that maintain the bad habits are in your mind.
2. Because you are getting a payoff for what you are presently doing, you are not likely to work on new tactics.

Let's look at these two points more closely:

Herb and Bonnie were enjoying a fine advanced hill. Dropping over a crest onto a steep pitch, Bonnie skied beautifully through some deep snow between the trees. In contrast, Herb literally stopped in his tracks, looking for a way around. Not finding one, he slowly skied the rest of the pitch. His body was stiff and he fought to keep his balance.

To Herb, the payoff was that he avoided falling and also lessened his feelings of apprehension. By skiing slowly, stiffly, and miserably, he succeeded this time. As for Bonnie, however, it never occurred to her to slow down because her earlier emotional learning was somewhat different—there were no payoffs for slowing down.

The second point is also illustrated in the above example. Herb didn't try anything new! Bonnie was yelling at him to face more downhill, but he was still twisted back into the hill, feeling safer that way. He was angry at himself, but at least he wasn't falling and he was feeling safer. Had he relaxed his muscles and looked ahead, he would have done better. When you try new things for the first time, they will always feel a little odd and you will be unstable, which may give you even more reason to revert to the bad habit. Essentially you have been punished for trying something new! It is hard to convince your mind that nothing ventured is nothing gained.

If you doubt our analysis thus far, ask yourself why so many bad habits seem almost universal. Emotional and operant learning are taking place and interacting. We will say it again: Skiing is not natural. What is natural is your response to a loss of equilibrium and the resultant learning of the bad habits we all seem to share at one time or another. This is a part of your psychology that *Skiing Out of Your Mind* is designed to change.

Vicarious Fear: The Downside of Learning by Looking

Almost everything you learn by direct personal experience can also be learned by watching other people. There is an abundance of solid evidence in the scientific literature that we can and do learn both operantly and emotionally by observing others.

Susan had just skied an intermediate run in and out of some chopped-up powder. She was feeling great, practically alone on that part of the mountain. Stopping at the intersection of two intermediate trails, she watched three reasonably good skiers take falls on a pitch just ahead. They were visibly shaken by the experience. Susan skied cautiously and tensely down that pitch, looking for all the world like a be-

ginner not enjoying herself. Yet the pitch was no steeper, no bumpier, no choppier than the stretch she had just finished.

What happened was that Susan had learned vicariously by watching several people model fear on that pitch. Her emotional self made her physical self tense in order to avoid falling. This is a fine example of the subtle ways in which we learn. Susan did not understand why she couldn't relax on the second pitch. She was unaware of the vicarious learning that had just taken place.

How about the good side? Can learning by observation really help? Absolutely and emphatically, yes! There are techniques to help you maximize the good and minimize the bad. (We'll review these in chapter 7, "Vicarious Learning: Learning by Looking.")

Getting Cold Feet

There is another negative side effect of feeling apprehensive when you ski. It is an aspect of the fear response that invariably goes unrecognized by skiers: Being scared or nervous when you ski tends to make your extremities more susceptible to cold. There is an interesting physiological basis for this phenomenon.

The part of your nervous system that is involved with feeling emotions, with involuntary bodily responses such as digestion and heart rate, and with preparing the body for action or relaxation is called the autonomic nervous system. It is divided into two physiologically distinguishable parts, the sympathetic and the parasympathetic. These two parts generally act in opposition to each other, the sympathetic sending out the impulses for your anxiety or emergency reactions and the parasympathetic sending out impulses associated with relaxation.

The sympathetic gets your body ready for something. Your heart rate speeds up, your breathing changes, your mouth gets dry, and a lot of blood is sent to your major muscle systems. When the blood gets shifted to your major muscles, the blood vessels in your extremities constrict, thus lowering the blood supply to your hands and feet. Naturally, when you experience anxiety and your peripheral blood vessels constrict, it will be more difficult to keep your extremities warm. The expression "getting cold feet" did not just pop up from nowhere. Because you are afraid, your sympathetic nervous system has called for a reduction in the blood flow to your feet while increasing that flow to your major muscles. Keeping your hands and feet moving helps, of course, but you are fighting your nervous system if you are anxious and trying to keep warm at the same time.

In contrast to the action of the sympathetic aspect of your autonomic nervous system, the parasympathetic is associated with relaxation. Among other things, the blood flow to the extremities increases when you are relaxed. In fact, some types of psychotherapy employ accurate measurement of skin temperature at the fingertips, both to assess the presence of anxiety and to help teach relaxation skills. If you ski psychologically relaxed, your hands and feet will probably stay warmer.

Notice we are not claiming that because you get cold hands or feet this proves you are fearful. (When you get really seriously chilled, there is an involuntary shift of blood to reduce heat loss in an effort to maintain an acceptable body-core temperature. This also involves a dramatic shift of blood from the extremities, but not because of anxiety.) We are saying that if you don't ski relaxed, however, not only will it be more difficult to ski well but you will be a lot colder in the process!

Conversations That Hurt Your Skiing

Let's turn to how talking to yourself has such a powerful effect on your skiing. Some portions of your brain that developed early in human evolution are most important in the physiological response to emotional experience. As strange as it may seem, it is quite difficult for those portions of your brain to distinguish between self-generated emotional input (like simply *talking* to yourself about fear) and input from your *external* environment. You can and do respond to your internal "fear-talk" about those sharp moguls in a manner very similar to external "fear-stimuli" (the actual moguls)! You can and do respond to anger with yourself and to self-punishment in a manner similar to punishment directed toward you by another person. That is why it is both physiologically and psychologically possible for your skiing to seriously suffer when you are your own worst enemy.

On Being
Your Own
Worst Enemy

The following is an experience one of us had a few years ago. It started as a 2-day stop at Steamboat Springs, Colorado. The first day was spectacular. The second could have been even better.

Ten inches of light power had fallen the night before. My friends and I awoke to a brilliant sun, rising above an ocean of sparkling snow. But...

The day began with a 10-minute wait for a breakfast table and a 30-minute wait for food. I started muttering to myself: "Powder's going to be tracked up. I should have gotten up sooner....Dammit, where is our food? There's no excuse for this kind of thing. I can't stand waiting for other people to do their job." My friends stayed relaxed and joked about the waiter.

After waiting 20 minutes in line, we got to the top of the mountain. The view was spectacular, the sky clear, but all I could focus on were the problems. I kept muttering to myself: "Snow's already tracked up....It's like an anthill up here....I'm a fool for not getting up earlier....My boots don't feel so hot, either." All of that in spite of the fact that only a dozen people were ahead of us on this particular run.

My friends stayed relaxed and smiled at me. We started down the mountain. I fell in the first hundred feet. I was enraged: "Damn bindings. Too many people, too."

*My friends had their rhythm. They were flowing beauti-
fully over and around the bumps. The powder was spectacular. They reluctantly stopped and waited a few hundred
yards down the mountain. Picking myself up, I skied fitfully
down to them and started complaining. I couldn't stand
myself or my skiing.*

*To make a painful story short, I continued with the same
attitude for the rest of the morning. By early afternoon, my
friends were telling me to get lost—I could yell at myself and
wallow in my own misery if I wished, but I was ruining their
skiing. I felt miserable, was totally insensitive to my body
and the terrain, and was getting worse with every run.*

You have probably heard the expression "be your own best
friend." It usually means to be good to yourself both physically
and mentally. It means having reasonable expectations, complimenting yourself, and talking to yourself in a positive way.
Each of these things improves the quality of your life. Each
also improves the quality of your skiing a great deal more than
you might think.

With distressing regularity, we neglect to be our own best
friend. Instead we become our own worst enemy—and not just
in skiing, either. Even on a day-to-day basis this is often one
of the biggest problems we create for ourselves. An increasing body of research and clinical literature in psychology is
concerned with modifying "worst enemy" habits. Skiing is
one of those areas where being our own worst enemy stands
out in bold relief. We get angry with ourselves. We talk
nonsense to ourselves. We frighten and punish ourselves.

To understand the unusual power of what you imagine and
say to yourself, you need to appreciate the fact that it is difficult for your autonomic nervous system to distinguish between the external world and the world you create in your
mind. Recall that your autonomic nervous system is
associated with your emotions and tends to respond to your
experiences automatically. It matters little to your autonomic
nervous system whether these experiences originate in your
external environment or your internal environment.
(Technically, they do not become experiences until you have
received and interpreted—talked to yourself—about your sensory input.) You can and frequently do talk yourself into feeling emotional. You have demonstrated that principle to

yourself many times. Recall the last time you felt jealous by simply thinking that someone special was with another person. Or recall how your mouth puckers when you think about a lemon, or how you feel aroused by sexual thoughts and images. All your feelings at such times are the responses of your autonomic nervous system to your self-talk and your images.

Conversations and Images

Actually there are at least two internal channels to which your autonomic nervous system will readily respond. Since they significantly influence your emotional responses while skiing, it is well worth defining them. Both are channels of imagining:

1. *Conversations* you have with yourself in your mind. These are called self-statements, self-talk, private monologues, or covert verbalizations. This is the verbal channel.
2. *Images* of events, most often visual or kinesthetic (feeling) but including the other senses as well. In skiing, for example, common problem images involve seeing or feeling yourself crossing your tips and crashing. This is the sensory channel.

It does not matter which channel you typically use. The important point is that your self-talk and images have an amazing influence on your feelings and behavior. *You* begin and continue the monologues and the images *on your own*. In fact, in skiing (as in living), we often set ourselves up for failure. The ideas behind the sayings "it's all in your mind" or "you're imagining things" are important in looking at human behavior. Recall the last time you were told, "Don't worry. It's all in your mind!" If you are like most people, that did not help your feelings in the least; you still worried.

There are two kinds of destructive mental imagery in which you may engage: (1) anger-images and the associated self-punishment, and (2) fear-images and the associated catastrophes.

It was race day and Jim had been building up to this for months. It was the most important race of the season. He woke up to discover it was snowing heavily and the mountain was shrouded in fog. He began recalling a horrible fall in a race under similar conditions. He got angry at himself just thinking about it and then began to get angry at the weather. "It's not fair that I have to race in these conditions." His concentration began to wane.

Debbie was a pro when it came to anger self-talk. She had perfected the art of the internal temper tantrum. A talented skier, she would occasionally lose control in deep powder and take a mild fall. Then, turning fun into misery, she would slam her pole down (sometimes losing it), and get so angry with herself that for the rest of the run the lightest powder would seem like cement: "What a fool I am! I just can't get this. What's wrong with me? I ought to be able to ski this. Come on, you jerk. Get it together."

Does this sound familiar? When skiers talk about psyching themselves out or letting their minds get in the way, they are talking about being their own worst enemy. You are your own worst enemy when your self-talk is angry, self-punishing, self-critical, or fearful. On the positive side, you are psyching yourself up when your self-talk is positive, rewarding, euphoric, or complimentary.

Anger and Self-Criticism

Consider how anger and harsh self-criticism can affect your skiing. To put it in perspective, try this brief exercise:

Recall an instance when you were angry with yourself. Precisely why were you so upset? If on skis, was it because you were not skiing up to your potential? Take a few minutes to sit back and recapture that anger. Reconstruct as accurately as possible your comments to yourself. What were you saying? How did you feel while you were condemning yourself? Were you swearing a lot?

Now, *repeat* it all to yourself. *Do it.* Recapture that self-talk. Create a wave of anger. Feel it. Hear yourself talking. Hear yourself swearing. You're angry at yourself. Stop reading for a moment and let it pour over you.

Now, turn it around. Recreating the feelings you have just had, ask yourself quite seriously how you would have reacted had someone else said the same thing to you in the same tone of voice, for the same reasons? Sit back and imagine it for a moment. How are you reacting? Feel like telling him or her to jump off a cliff?

To understand the effect that this type of imagining can have on your skiing, consider this carefully: *How long do you think you could or would remain friends with someone who criticized you as much as you do yourself?*

The Effects of Self-Punishment

Exactly what effects does self-punishment have on your skiing? It has some of the same effects that punishment does in general. It makes you feel terrible, both about yourself and your skiing, and it gives little information about the appropriate skiing strategy. This leaves you helpless to do anything different.

Bad feelings toward yourself create immediate problems, First of all, you may decide skiing is no fun. We wonder how many people are on the verge of giving up skiing, not because they get particularly cold or even because they fall often, but because they have made skiing so unpleasant for themselves by their self-punishment. Chances are you have not given up skiing completely or you wouldn't be reading this book. More than likely, only certain conditions or runs have become unpleasant. In any case you are pushing your arousal level up past the peak performance point. You are reacting to your internal private conversations with yourself and not to what is really happening out there. For example, no one is *really* yelling at you. Yet your autonomic nervous system does not know the difference. Therefore, your feelings don't either! To the degree that you are responding to your skiing with anger and self-punishment, skiing is controlling you. You are the effect of your skiing. That is obviously the reverse of how it should be.

In addition, self-punishment teaches you nothing new in terms of technique. When you get angry at yourself, just as when someone else punishes you strongly and consistently, you tend either to become paralyzed and do nothing or to respond randomly, trying anything that has even a remote chance of working.

Finally, you have not built in any payoffs for continuing good skiing tactics. You know well by now that with no payoffs, even parts of your skiing that are good will not likely continue. In fact, if you have a couple of excellent ski behaviors tucked in among the bad habits, and you tend to be a self-punishing person, the chances are that even the good habits will stagnate.

Self-Criticism and Standard-Setting

Your expectations or standards can be a source of some real problems. Failure to meet your expectations gives you cause for self-punishment.

Pete was always euphoric when he began a day of skiing. He personified the enthusiastic, optimistic recreational skier. He did have one problem, however: by early afternoon his optimism and enthusiasm were severely strained, and on the last run he was like the grinch who stole weekends. What's worse, he couldn't figure out how he lost his enthusiasm every day.

His problem was a common one. Pete, it seemed, would start off the day saying he was going to ski every run with what he liked to call "flowing aggression": "I will not get tense. I will flow over every bump, setting edges, carving turns, rarely falling. My legs will be like shock absorbers."

But he never achieved flowing aggression. How could he expect to? This was only his second season on skis! Although he was a good athlete, he had a lot to learn about technique before his skiing could flow at all. As a result of repeated failures to meet his expectations, he began to get angry, then depressed, and finally he felt like giving up altogether.

Standards. The word sounds innocuous enough. In fact, however, it is inextricably tied in with the entire self-criticism issue. Our standards influence the way we view the world and ourselves. Some of us fail to meet our standards once in a while. Others fail much of the time. The difference in "failure" rates lies not so much in skill levels as in our own goal-setting process. It is the standards you set for yourself that determine how successful you are. If your expectations are unrealistic, you will fail often. You become a self-punisher *and yet you set the standards equally high the next time.* You predictably "fail," go through your now-familiar self-criticism routine, and let your skiing *control you* in the next 50 feet as well.

You pay a high price for your expectations. Regardless of whether you are a novice or an advanced skier, your standards can still block you from achieving your peak performance. As you respond to your repeated perceptions of failure, you effectively block any reasonable chance for efficient learning. You give yourself no new information about skiing. Furthermore, *you are not having any fun.*

Fear and Catastrophizing

"The only thing we have to fear is fear itself." President Franklin D. Roosevelt's famous quote is as applicable to skiing as it was to the economic crisis of the Depression. Fear is a response of the autonomic nervous system to external or internal (self-generated) stimuli. The effects of fear on your skiing are now familiar:

- Fear often gets attached to certain skiing conditions (emotional learning) and makes you insensitive to your body, your skis, and the terrain.
- The reduction of your fear is the payoff for avoiding new tactics (recall chapter 2).
- Fear feels terrible!

We have not yet discussed some problems with the self-generation of fear, which has a lot to do with raising your arousal past your optimum (peak) performance level. Why do the same external situations, certain ski conditions for example, affect one person and not another? Why do some skiers love fresh powder on steep hills while others quake in their boots when faced with the identical situation?

Much of the answer lies in the *self-generating* process: The Stoic philosophers of ancient Greece did not have to be skiers to observe that *we respond to the world as we perceive it to be, not as it objectively exists.* Look at a field of big, steep moguls. Are you frightened or challenged? It is clearly the same mogul field either way. The *moguls* are not primarily responsible for making you feel scared or challenged. In large part, *you* are. Let us shed some light on our self-generation of fear.

Just as in the self-punishment process, internal fear-talk will be provoked by your interpretation of certain conditions in your environment. The self-punishment cycle may be set in motion after setting a goal and "failing"; the fear-talk may come from just momentarily losing your balance, actually falling, seeing another skier falling, or simply by just imagining that you're falling. At that point you will begin to catastrophize. The process of catastrophizing involves thoughts and images about what *might* happen or *could have* happened (broken legs, broken skis?).

Catastrophizing is self-defeating in that you are attaching labels and emotions to ski conditions and terrain before you even get there. As you are lying after a fall on the lee side of a mogul, you are not fearful because you just fell. You have already fallen, so there is nothing to be afraid of. Rather, your fear is that you might again fall in the next hundred feet. Perhaps you are rehearsing in your mind what could have happened (the "whew-that-could-have-been-an-absolute-disaster" routine) and are responding to that.

It's Not All Bad

Lest you have the impression that all internal talk is bad, we want to make it clear that it can be equally powerful when you use it to your advantage. *Skiing Out of Your Mind* does not mean that you are under the control of your skis; it means that your skis, and your mind, are under *your* control. The influence of your self-statements, images, and perceptions is powerful. The techniques covered in the forthcoming chapters will teach you to use that influence to your advantage.

Active Awareness and Being Your Own Personal Scientist

Many years ago, when travel in northern New England was accomplished by narrow two-lane roads, a New York ski enthusiast was driving to Stowe, Vermont, for a weekend of spring skiing. Never having traveled these roads before, he was worried about losing his way. His anxieties were realized when he came to an unmarked fork in the road next to an old general store. Fortunately, a weathered Vermonter, his corncob pipe smoldering in his mouth, was sitting on the porch of the store. "Old man!" hailed the New Yorker. "Which way to Stowe?" "Well, sir," the Vermonter replied in his best Yankee accent, "you best take the right fork and go up to the four corners. Head north and uh....Nope, on second thought, better take the left fork and go up to the next village.... Whoa, that ain't right either. You better take this road on back to the covered bridge and head east till you....Nope, come to think of it, Mister, you can't get there from here!"

Skiing without awareness is like putting yourself in the hands of the old Vermonter. You may think you know where you want to go, but you do not know where you are and you are not likely to find a way of getting there. Active awareness is what distinguishes the conscious skier from the mindless one. It is what allows you to take charge of your skiing, to look at it, see it, and make it yours. In short, it is what allows you to become the cause of your skiing rather than the effect of it.

Active awareness consists of knowing and understanding where you are now and knowing and understanding where you want to go in both your skiing and your ski psychology. It is learning to realistically assess your skiing. It is learning to hear yourself think, to figure out what triggers your psych-outs, and to develop an increased sense of your body. It is also learning to set and work toward manageable, measurable goals. Active awareness is a central theme of *Skiing Out of Your Mind.*

Self-Assessment: Awareness of Your Ski Psychology

The following statements are designed to help you look at your use of psychological techniques in improving skiing performance. They are designed to help you increase your awareness of where you stand in terms of applying psychological techniques to your skiing. The statements come from various chapters of this book, and after you take the test you should have a better idea of what chapters might be of special use to you. Please grade each statement as honestly as possible by using the following rating scale:

1 = Not at all descriptive of me. Just doesn't apply.
2 = Not particularly descriptive of me. Only true 15% of the time.
3 = Yes, 30% of the time.
4 = About 50-50.
5 = Yes, 70% of the time.
6 = Quite descriptive of me. True 85% of the time.
7 = Very descriptive of me. True most all of the time.

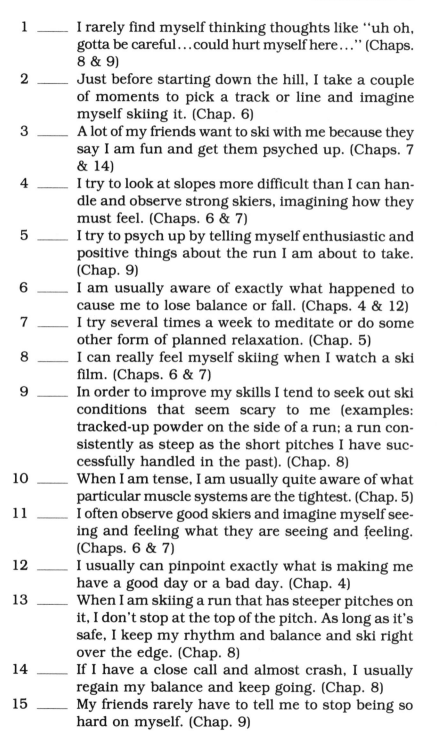

1 _____ I rarely find myself thinking thoughts like "uh oh, gotta be careful...could hurt myself here..." (Chaps. 8 & 9)

2 _____ Just before starting down the hill, I take a couple of moments to pick a track or line and imagine myself skiing it. (Chap. 6)

3 _____ A lot of my friends want to ski with me because they say I am fun and get them psyched up. (Chaps. 7 & 14)

4 _____ I try to look at slopes more difficult than I can handle and observe strong skiers, imagining how they must feel. (Chaps. 6 & 7)

5 _____ I try to psych up by telling myself enthusiastic and positive things about the run I am about to take. (Chap. 9)

6 _____ I am usually aware of exactly what happened to cause me to lose balance or fall. (Chaps. 4 & 12)

7 _____ I try several times a week to meditate or do some other form of planned relaxation. (Chap. 5)

8 _____ I can really feel myself skiing when I watch a ski film. (Chaps. 6 & 7)

9 _____ In order to improve my skills I tend to seek out ski conditions that seem scary to me (examples: tracked-up powder on the side of a run; a run consistently as steep as the short pitches I have successfully handled in the past). (Chap. 8)

10 _____ When I am tense, I am usually quite aware of what particular muscle systems are the tightest. (Chap. 5)

11 _____ I often observe good skiers and imagine myself seeing and feeling what they are seeing and feeling. (Chaps. 6 & 7)

12 _____ I usually can pinpoint exactly what is making me have a good day or a bad day. (Chap. 4)

13 _____ When I am skiing a run that has steeper pitches on it, I don't stop at the top of the pitch. As long as it's safe, I keep my rhythm and balance and ski right over the edge. (Chap. 8)

14 _____ If I have a close call and almost crash, I usually regain my balance and keep going. (Chap. 8)

15 _____ My friends rarely have to tell me to stop being so hard on myself. (Chap. 9)

16 ＿＿ In most sports I have learned, I have found that I often practice in my mind even when not engaging in the sport. (Chap. 6)

17 ＿＿ In skiing, the only things I can control are myself and my skis, so I usually just try to adapt to the conditions. (Chap. 9)

18 ＿＿ My idea of competing is to ski to the very best of my ability and let the outcome take care of itself. (Appendix B)

19 ＿＿ When my friends want to ski more difficult runs than I do, I am comfortable saying "No thanks, I'll just go ahead and meet you a little later." (Chap. 13)

20 ＿＿ When riding the lift, I pay much more attention to skiers who are skiing well than to those who are skiing poorly. (Chap. 7)

21 ＿＿ When I find myself thinking self-critical thoughts, I stop them and rethink things in a more constructive way. (Chap. 9)

22 ＿＿ I am able to enjoy and ski safely in flat light by being very aware of my feet and legs and sensing the terrain beneath me. (Chap. 4)

23 ＿＿ When I am at the top of a difficult pitch or race course, I will imagine myself skiing it and get that feeling in my body before I start. (Chap. 6)

24 ＿＿ It usually doesn't bother me to have people watch me from a lift. (Chaps. 9 & 15)

25 ＿＿ When I lose my concentration, I am able to get it back. (Chap. 10)

26 ＿＿ When I find myself on terrain that is beyond my ability, I am able to pause, relax, and cope with my fear. (Chap. 13)

27 ＿＿ When I ski to a stop, I make a point of turning and stopping to my weak side as often as to my strong side. (Chap. 8)

28 ＿＿ When I go out to ski, I generally have a specific goal in mind, whether to learn something new, have fun, or whatever. (Chap. 4)

29 ＿＿ I have learned and often use metaphors when I ski (examples: imagining lights on my knees pointing to where I want to go, or imagining slithering through the bumps like a snake). (Chap. 11)

30 _____ When I face a difficult obstacle in my skiing, I can believe in my ability to overcome the obstacle. (Chap. 15)

Total your score. The higher the number, the more understanding you seem to have of psychological techniques. However, there is no correct grade. As you review your scores, pay special attention to statements for which you had particularly low scores. Each statement corresponds to a particular chapter in the book. Although we recommend that you read the entire book, we suggest that you return to those chapters on which you had low scores.

Pinpointing Where You Are and Where You Want to Go

Consider for a moment two or three aspects of your skiing you would like to improve. But be realistic. Your goals should be specific enough to be manageable. There are two reasons for this: First, if you cannot accurately specify the improvements you would like to make, you will only be able to guess which tactics to use for change. And if your attempts at improvement stem from guesswork, you will still be a victim of the unfocused and unconscious learning that taught you your bad habits in the first place. Second, if you cannot specify your goals enough to keep track of them, you will not know whether you are improving. Thus it will be easy for you to get discouraged, feel like giving up, and go back to being your own worst enemy.

If your goals are to be a racer or to ski bumps better, you have plenty of company, but these goals are too vague. What aspects of being a racer? Better than what? Almost all of us tend to make our standards too vague and set them too high. We defeat ourselves before we begin. This is how we set ourselves up to be our own worst enemies.

Carol was not satisfied with her skiing. She had a minor injury early in her first season. Her second and third seasons were totally fear-dominated. Her goal was to not be afraid.

There is no doubt that Carol had a problem with fear. But her definition of the problem was not adequate. Fear of what? Speed? Bumps? Ice? Being hurt? Should she have included internal fear-talk? How about her tendency to sit down and cry when things go badly? When you pinpoint a problem area, you need to be specific. The following is a much better account of Carol's skiing and ski psychology:

Since she had injured her leg shortly after losing control one day, she could vividly imagine it happening again. In fact, she began thinking about it a couple of days before planned ski weekends, occasionally imagined it while riding the lift, and consistently reminded herself how long it had taken to recover from the injury. While on the hill she fought every small gain in speed by long traverses. Her goals were to ski more aggressively while on easy hills and stop rehearsing the potential catastrophes that served only to scare her.

Notice how much more workable her problem is here. Notice also that both her skiing and ski psychology are being carefully considered. Further clarifying "more aggressively," she defined it as "skiing a little faster and more down the fall line." What she meant by "scaring" herself were her internal statements about loss of control and leg injuries. This was something she could monitor easily by paying attention to her self-talk.

Here is another example:

Jim was a good, aggressive skier. His technique was sound, and in general he was happy with his skiing. Most of his friends looked to him as an excellent skier, except that he fell a lot. His goal was to ski from the top to the bottom of any typical advanced run under conditions of chopped-up snow without falling.

This is a specific goal, but it does not provide information about how to reach it. Jim could certainly monitor whether or not he fell, but what would he learn about how he did it? What specific problem prevented him from skiing top to bottom without falling? By not properly defining and working with those specific problems—a common error skiers make when wanting to improve—Jim did two things. First, he learned little about what his problems really were and therefore what strategies to use on them. Second, he set standards that were too high for his initial efforts. As he failed to meet those standards he increasingly became his own worst enemy. Under those conditions, he began to defeat himself in the truest sense of the words. He needed to develop more awareness of his falling.

Jim observed that he was falling backward most of the time. He found he was not particularly fearful but was quite embarrassed to ski like that in front of his friends. He was also extremely angry at himself. He would have internal temper tantrums every time he fell. He was stiffening up and losing track of his weight distribution.

Armed with this reasonable analysis of the problem, he modified his goal. First he resolved to work on his self-statements of embarrassment and anger, and second to begin each run with a few relaxed turns before increasing the aggressive dimension of his skiing.

Here are a few more examples of definitions that are realistic and specific:

- typically avoiding steeper hills,
- sitting too far back on your skis,
- not flexing your legs,
- telling yourself how stupid you are,
- burying your tips in powder,
- traversing too much,
- rehearsing how fearful you are in bumps.

Examples of nonspecific definitions are:

- losing it in bumps,
- being afraid,
- wanting to ski better,
- wanting to look better.

In order to develop active awareness regarding your present position and your goals, you start with general impressions from your experience and refine them down to specific, manageable problems. It is like being your own personal scientist. You will be amazed at how many of your problems can be distilled into something workable. And you will be delighted to find out how much easier it is to improve when you have some specifics on which to focus. It is like the difference between telling the doctor, "I don't feel well," and telling him or her, "I have a pain in the lower right part of my abdomen that gets worse when I move." The doctor's task is much easier in the latter case.

Take a moment to review the need for active awareness. If you are not conscientious at this point, the rest of your effort will be jeopardized. You might try a couple of times, fail to change at all, throw this book in the trash basket, and give up. You will of course have acted predictably. Why continue when there is no payoff? We are very much aware of this potential problem; that is why we put so much emphasis on being conscientious.

Awareness of Your Skiing Contexts

Now that you have set realistic goals and identified an aspect of your skiing that you want to improve, you must expand your awareness of the problem by analyzing the context in which it occurs. Here we ask you to pay particular attention to your ski psychology. You need to understand the contexts in order to change your skiing.

Your skiing has two contexts, outer and inner. The outer context includes all those aspects of your external environment that influence the way you ski and the way you think. Examples are:

- the snow,
- the light and weather,
- the terrain,
- people,
- your clothes,
- your skis.

The inner context includes everything you carry around with you that also influences how you ski and how you think:

* your thoughts (cognitions),
* your images,
* your body sensations,
* your emotions.

Different contexts produce different problems in your skiing and require different solutions. Recall that Jim (in the previous section) was falling a lot. He focused on the outer context to discover what precipitated his falls:

For Jim, chopped-up fresh snow resulted in frequent falls. It also evoked feelings of embarrassment. By paying attention to his skiing and his falling he made an interesting discovery: He fell a lot more when he was skiing with other good skiers. (As you might expect, his feelings of embarrassment were also greater when his friends were present.)

When Jim turned his attention to the inner context of his falling, he became aware of a pressure to show off for others. While his body was contending with the terrain, his mind was focused on who was watching him. Out of the corner of his eye he would check to see if people were looking at him. Jim realized that he was not skiing the mountain, he was trying to ski the crowd.

It is easy to let yourself become the victim of your skiing. If you are in that psychological place, you have surrendered all of your control to outer contexts such as gravity, weather, and terrain, and to the vagaries of your inner context (an unfocused mind or a mind focused on self-defeating thoughts and images). The way to reassert control is to develop awareness about how you function in response to your contexts. Then you are in a place of awareness and knowledge and moving toward a place of coping and control. Once the context of a problem becomes clear, a variety of solutions can unfold that are based upon the tactics covered in the forthcoming chapters.

Kinesthetic Awareness:
Staying in Touch With Yourself

Most of us have difficulty skiing in flat light. This lack of vision is disorienting at the least. For some skiers it is almost disabling. We need to see to ski, or so we believe. Yet, downhill racers hit speeds in excess of 80 mph in flat light, and there are hundreds of blind skiers! How do they do it?

Consider blind skiers. With their guides, they hear and *feel* their way down. They do not need to see to ski because their auditory and kinesthetic senses are highly tuned. By *kinesthetic* we mean that sense you have of your body in motion and space. For sighted people, skiing is a strongly *visual-kinesthetic* activity. Often, however, we rely too heavily on the vision part, to the relative exclusion of feeling our body positions and movements as we ski. Blind skiers represent a peak of kinesthetic awareness. Top racers represent that same peak...and at breakneck speeds.

Kinesthetic awareness is like having a mirror in your mind that reflects your sense of where your body is and where it is moving. Without it you have little information about whether you are skiing the way you think you are. Also, without kinesthetic awareness there is a large gap in the mental imagery available to you for practice. In other words, you are literally quite blind to an essential source of information. In skiing, a finely tuned kinesthetic sense enables you to compare your actual movements with your intended movements.

The following exercises are designed to help you polish your mental mirror and see more clearly into your body. The general pattern of these exercises follows a four-step sequence, the same sequence as the one you will learn to use to recall and "wire-in" your best skiing experiences (chapter 6).

1. Make an attempt to mentally rehearse each exercise before you begin. We will be discussing mental rehearsal further, so for now we are asking you just to make that attempt. Some of you will be quite good at creating a mental image of how your muscles feel and your joints flex;

others will find it difficult to imagine kinesthetically. That is ok. You will find it instructive in either case. This first step can be considered a "before" snapshot.

2. Excess tension blocks awareness of the gentle aspects of skiing. This is a good place to begin learning to identify tension areas in your body. Let go of them, as best you can, before you do the exercise.

3. Do the exercise following the instructions given.

4. Explore the "afterimage" of the exercise. Take a moment with your eyes closed to review the exercise just completed, comparing this afterimage to the before snapshot.

To help you increase your kinesthetic awareness, we are taking an approach that gives you carefully structured practice in relying less on vision and more on feel. At times you will be skiing with your eyes closed, so these exercises should be done with a partner, on an uncrowded groomed slope with which you are familiar.

The exercises become more challenging in what we think is an easy progression. But do not consider them cast in blue ice. If you are an advanced skier and the steps are too small, by all means jump ahead. If they are too big, make up your own to put in between. And if you would prefer to start these exercises with "impaired" vision instead of skiing with your eyes closed, feel free to move ahead a couple of pages to the section on impaired vision skiing and then come back to this section.

Skiing in the Dark

Skiing in the dark requires that you close your eyes before each of the following steps. If you feel that you are getting into trouble, you can always sneak a peek.

Standing and Walking

1. Flex your left leg, bringing the ski completely off the snow. Focus on the feeling of this movement. Notice how you balance on one ski. What are your arms doing? Your shoulders? Your head? Extend your leg till the ski just

barely touches the snow. What part of the ski touched first? Last?

2. Repeat the above with your right leg, noticing the same muscle systems. Also notice if your sense of balance is different.

3. On flat terrain, walk ahead, noticing how your skis slide. Also notice small terrain variations and how they feel to you.

Traversing For the following exercises, please make sure you are on an uncrowded groomed slope with a partner acting as traffic cop and your eyes.

1. Have your partner stand about 15 yards slightly downhill from you. Look toward her/him, examining the terrain between the two of you. You will attempt to stop near your partner. Instruct him/her to give you feedback as you ski, on your stance, balance, posture, and so forth. Begin with a shallow traverse, one that will allow you to slide without poling but not pick up too much speed. Now close your eyes. Push off. Use your feet and legs as sensors between your mind and the terrain. Notice any changes in speed and terrain, and how your body maintains balance. Do you compensate with your legs? Your arms? Are you standing comfortably in a natural, erect posture or are you bent at the waist? Is your upper body tilted into the hill? Do your skis slip sideways? What do you hear? Does what you feel correspond to what your partner is telling you?

2. Repeat the traverse in the other direction. Remember to have your partner watch out for traffic and keep you informed. Did you feel more comfortable going in this direction? Less comfortable? What are the differences, if any?

3. Repeat the traverses until you feel, and your partner confirms, that you are standing and skiing as you thought you were.

4. When you feel comfortable with flat traverses, gradually make them steeper. When you feel comfortable with that and you can come to a stop easily at the point you are aiming for, you are ready to take a few straight runs.

Straight Runs

1. On a very gentle groomed slope, have your partner stand downhill from you about 20 yards away. Close your eyes and do a quick tension check. When your partner gives you the all-clear, push off. Pay attention to your body and the terrain. How are you standing? Are you skiing the way you usually ski with your eyes open? If not, what's different? How are you controlling your speed? Stop. Open your eyes. How did you stop? Did you use a wedge? Turn uphill? Hockey stop? Compare your mental picture of your run with your partner's feedback.

2. Repeat, coming to a stop first by using a wedge, then by turning uphill, then by doing a hockey stop. How close were you to your partner? Are you getting more familiar with yourself?

Turning

1. When you feel comfortable with straight runs, it's time to do turns. Make sure you are on an uncrowded, groomed, gentle run with your partner acting as a traffic cop and feedback monitor. Close your eyes. With your partner alongside, you will ski downhill. The important thing here is to get a rhythm going and keep it going till you stop. Your partner should signal you to stop when you have gone about 30 yards, or before if necessary. As you are keeping your turns going as long as you can, notice how your body reacts to changes in terrain and snow. If you lose your balance, regain it. If you fall, stop for a moment to review your kinesthetic experience just prior to and during the fall, and begin again. (If you fall repeatedly, you're probably not ready to do turns with your eyes closed, or you may be on a slope too difficult for you. Go back to shallower terrain, or go back to the traversing and straight running exercises for a few more tries.)

    Review your run. What kinds of turns were you making? Short radius, medium, or long? Were you in a wedge, wide track, narrow track? Did you turn more easily to one side? How does what you felt compare with what your partner saw?

2. Repeat the turning exercise, but this time decide on the kinds of turns you will make and the techniques you will use ahead of time, and inform your partner of these so you can get feedback from him or her.

Impaired Vision Skiing

If you have been skiing with your eyes closed, this exercise will be surprisingly easy. If you have not, you will find this to be very rewarding and quite revealing. It should be done on an uncrowded groomed slope, one with which you are comfortable and can ski well. You should have a partner both for safety and feedback.

Smooth Terrain

1. At the top of your intended run, scan the slope and plan where you will ski, what kinds of turns you will make and, if you wish, where you will make your first two or three turns. Close your eyes and push off. Now, blink your eyes open as briefly as you can, much like the shutter on a camera. Continue skiing, blinking your eyes open momentarily as you turn. Establish a rhythm and keep it going until you reach your stopping point.

    What did you discover about how much you use your eyes when you ski? When we have asked people to do impaired vision skiing, we (and they) have been most surprised at how little time their eyes were open. They blinked quickly and much less frequently than expected.

2. After gaining experience with exercise 1, repeat it several times and pay particular attention to your body when your eyes are closed. How does it react to changes in terrain and snow? Do you notice any slight shifts in your stance front to back? Side to side? Are you absorbing small bumps? How? With your legs, by flexing your knees and hips? With your lower back? Are you remaining relatively inflexible and being jarred by them? Are you flexing your legs smoothly throughout the turn, or are you staying in one position? Do you extend your legs at the start of each new turn? What do these movements feel like? What did you hear? Finally, what kind of feedback are you getting from your partner?

Bumpy Terrain Start this exercise on bumps you can easily ski with your eyes open, working your way up to more difficult ones. Make sure the traffic warrants it, and that you have a partner acting as a traffic cop. The points to note are your balancing movements, your leg flexion and extension, where you are opening your eyes, and where you feel comfortable about keeping them closed.

1. Choose your bump run and start at one side of the hill so that you can traverse it. With your eyes closed, push off. Blink your eyes open briefly as you cross the hill, then stop at the other side. Do a series of these traverses in both directions, paying attention to your balancing movements and your flexion and extension. Open your eyes at various places: as you flex up, at the top of the bump, and as you extend down.
2. For advanced skiers only, begin now to link several turns. Begin with two or three linked turns, then get your line and ski it. Blink your eyes open as needed, but now pay careful attention to the contexts under which you need to see. Is it at turn initiation? Turn completion? At some kinesthetic cue, such as feeling your ski tips begin to come up?

Impaired Vision Gates

If you are a racer and you feel comfortable with skiing in the dark, you can begin to ski gates with your eyes closed. When we first suggest this exercise in our workshops, people respond with, "What! Are you nuts?"

If some such thought crossed your mind, consider this: Coming out of the start, you usually don't look at the first gate. In fact, in the course you seldom look at the gate you're approaching, and if you do, you know you're in trouble! So closing your eyes through the first gate should not be too difficult.

The "gates" we are talking about are not the usual bamboo. They're not really gates at all, but only markers in the snow such as spray dye or ribbons. You will ski mostly with your eyes closed, blinking them open only momentarily just as you did in the above exercises.

A Few Gates in the Dark   Have companions stationed along the course as gatekeepers both for safety and as a source of feedback. From the start, look at the first "gate," then past it. Focus on the first gate again, shift to the second, and then the third. Close your eyes, push off, and then open your eyes when you pass the first gate. Were you in the groove, skiing automatically? If so, you probably made it just fine. Keep working on this, two or three gates at a time, paying attention to how quickly you can get into the groove with your eyes closed, following your line by way of kinesthetic feedback alone. You will probably recognize this as excellent exercise for your mental imagery skills as well. Feel free to use it for this purpose, but be aware that we will be covering imagery material in detail in chapter 6 and Appendix C.

Blinking Through the Entire Course   Again, have companions stationed along the course. From the start, prepare and ski just as you normally do, only close your eyes before you push off. See where you are by blinking open your eyes. When you reach the finish, review your run. Compare your sensations of skiing with open eyes to skiing with closed eyes. How much did you actually have to see? How long could you go before having to see again?

If you complete and practice this exercise series you should expect significant improvement in your kinesthetic awareness. You will be more aware of how your skiing is affected by what you see and hear; you will become more sensitive to the terrain and snow through your feet, your visualization skills will be enhanced, and you will probably have less trouble the next time you ski in flat light.

Active Awareness and Centered Arousal

Recall the inverted U of the performance/arousal curve in chapter 1. Your performance is a function of your arousal, and if you have too little or too much arousal your performance is not at its best. There is a center for each of us on the curve. It is important that your active awareness include some sense of where your center is, as well as an ability to be aware of your arousal level as you are skiing.

There are three systems through which we experience arousal. Clinical psychologists call them "response systems" and classify them as cognitive, behavioral, and physiological. They interact constantly, and their relative contribution varies from person to person in any given situation. Taken together they make up an experience. Depending upon the circumstances, you might label that experience excitement, apprehension, aggression, fear, joy, or whatever. Let's look at what occurs in each of these response systems.

Cognitive

The material we discussed in chapter 3 on being your own worst enemy is largely cognitive. The cognitive system consists of self-statements expressed in either a verbal or image mode. It may be a conscious analysis of a problem or a way in which you are talking to yourself as the going gets rough. The cognitive system provides the labels for our physiological experience. That is, should your heart begin to beat quickly at the top of a steep bump run, you might experience that as fear or excitement, depending upon what you are saying to yourself. It is also the cognitive system that provides images of skiing beautifully or of possible catastrophes, images of winning your race, and images of the race course as you try to memorize it before your run. The following are examples:

- "Let me take this one step at a time."
- "This is far too steep for me. Feels awful."
- "What's the matter with me?"
- "Outstanding line through those bumps!"
- Image of winning your race.

Physiological

Your heart may be beating, your mouth dry, your pupils dilated, or your stomach may have butterflies. You may feel tense. Alternatively, your body may be feeling quite peaceful. The physiological system of arousal is the *fact* of what is going on inside your body. It can exist apart from conscious cognitive events, but it can also be a result of cognitive events (for example, talking to yourself in anger will cause your physiology to respond).

To be aware of your physiology, you observe, without labeling, how your body is responding. In the forthcoming chapters we tell you what to do with that information. At this point in developing your active awareness, the important thing is to include your physiological responses in your assessment. Following are examples of active awareness of your physiology:

- "My heart is beating fast."
- "I wasn't breathing on that bump run."
- "There goes my jaw, with that reflexive tightening."

Behavioral

Your cognitions and your physiology get translated into behavior (and vice versa). Awareness of your behavior means honing your ability to observe how you are acting in any particular situation. For example, do you find yourself avoiding bump runs (avoidance behavior)? Do you spend a great deal of time leaning into the hill and traversing (again, a type of avoidance behavior)? Do you seek out opportunities for competition? Do you bend your knees and pressure your skis when appropriate? These are all behaviors, and they are influenced by both what is going on inside your body and by what you interpret to be going on in the world outside your body. Examples of awareness of your behavior include these:

- "I'm over-rotating my shoulders."
- "I'm sitting too far back."
- "I extended my legs on that last bump run."
- "I held my edges on that icy section."

Integration of the Three Systems

It is obvious that these systems are inseparable in real life. When you feel your physiology reacting, you label the experience and perhaps adjust your behavior accordingly. When you behave, you observe yourself behaving, and quite frequently cognitive and physiological events follow. When you are thinking certain thoughts, your behavior will follow as directed and again some physiological experience will occur.

The ability to separate these channels just enough to be aware of their relative contribution to your present level of arousal comes with practice. You may need to increase your arousal in one system and at the same time decrease it in another! This is probably more true of competitive skiers who might need to use relaxation to quiet their physiology and at the same time increase their mental imagery of the race course about to be run.

More Than Only "Going For It"

Now that we have raised your active awareness and maybe stimulated considerable thought about your ski psychology, we would like to caution you against a couple of things most of us do when we apply psychological change principles.

First, once you have identified two or three weaknesses in your skiing and have described them clearly, choose the one that is the easiest to work on. If you are like most of us, you will probably want to tackle the hardest one first. That would be setting yourself up for failure again. There is no need to create frustration for yourself. Yet, some people insist on doing just that by attempting to ski over their heads instead of with their heads. For example, we have a friend with that attitude who is determined to master skiing big moguls. Every chance he has, he takes off for the biggest field of moguls he can find and literally beats his brains out against them. So far, the score is Bumps—50, Brains—0.

Another common mistake you may make in wanting to improve your skiing is that you may try to change everything at once. Think back to the last time you took a lesson or read a book about skiing. The next time you went skiing you probably told yourself several things to remember on your first run: "Keep your knees flexed. Don't stiffen your downhill leg. Hands forward. Weight on your downhill ski. Hips and shoulders square. Don't lean into the hill. Angulate. Get forward on the steep. Use your edges." And so on. So much chatter was going on in your mind that you probably had one of your worst days.

In order for your body to respond, your mind needs to be focused, but not obsessively. That would only result in what we call *analysis paralysis*. You cannot over-analyze, and you cannot be trying to accomplish six things at once. This principle is so simple and so obvious that we often forget it. The easiest way to maintain a single focus is to take one step at a time. Choose one problem to work on first. Only when you are satisfied with your improvement should you start on another problem. As you build on your improvements, the overall structure of your skiing will take shape. It is like building a house. Imagine what the stucture of your house would be if you tried to lay the foundation, hang the Sheetrock, paint the walls, and wire it—all at the same time.

Be Your Own Personal Scientist

Skiing Out of Your Mind requires careful sensing, careful thought, and a reasoned exploration of your problems. By developing awareness about the way you are skiing now, both with your body and with your mind, you can identify what works and what does not. To change what doesn't work into what does, you will need to apply physical, emotional, and cognitive relearning procedures. This process will let you become what sport psychologist Dr. Mike Mahoney calls your own "personal scientist." As such, you will be exploring the mind-body relationships in your own experience. You also will be changing your mind and body habits to bring your skiing more under your own control. The remainder of this book focuses on that process.

One last word about being your own personal scientist. Science, whether personal or universal, can become boring if it is approached mechanically and without curiosity. Or, it can be exciting and stimulating if it is approached with an enthusiasm for discovery. As you begin to explore your mind and your skiing, adopt an attitude of curiosity. If you find yourself losing interest, it is probably because you have lost that curiosity about your skiing. We have discovered that whenever we become bored with our skiing it is because we have already become bored with our psychology. We are either trying to force our bodies to do something our minds are not ready for or we have stopped being active with our minds. You can discover a great deal about how your mind affects your skiing and what you can do to affect your mind. Don't push it—that leads to anxiety. Don't become unconscious about it—that leads to passivity. Take an interest in it. Let your curiosity make a sport out of psychology, and you will be on the verge of making rewarding progress in your skiing!

Relaxation: Body and Mind

Recall the performance/arousal curve in chapter 1. Some arousal is good because it helps you to perform at your peak. However, often the problem in skiing is not that you need more arousal but that you need less. You may ski perfectly on a gentle, groomed slope and then fall apart (or fall down) when you hit bumps, ice, or a steep pitch. As we explained in chapter 2, this results from the natural reflexive tension of your mind and body when you encounter something difficult or fearful. You cannot ski well if you are too aroused.

If you are a competitive skier, the same thing applies to your racing. Perhaps you know what it is like to be skiing well in practice all week and yet freeze when you get into the starting gate on race day. You are so tense that you ski as if you were the unoiled Tin Man in "The Wizard of Oz." And it feels like it takes you about as long to get to the finish as it took him to get to Oz! Whether you are a racer or a recreational skier, being able to relax under stressful conditions would be a useful skill to have.

We want to emphasize that relaxation is a skill. This means two things: First, like any other skiing skill, it must be learned to be effective. One does not just stand in a starting gate and say, "Okay self, relax now." It is a skill that comes with practice both on and off the mountain. Second, relaxation is an integral part of all sport psychology programs but it is still only a tool. It is a building block upon which many of the psychological techniques in the forthcoming chapters are based. The ability to relax has been shown to enhance both your learning and performance of the psychological techniques used in *Skiing Out of Your Mind*.

Muscle Relaxation

Relax? That sounds easy enough, but what happens when you try to do it? For most people nothing happens. "I don't know what to do," they moan. Other people really try, but they just become more tense. Paradoxically, there is *nothing* to do to relax. Relaxation occurs by *not* trying. Unfortunately, most people don't know how to not try. The only time they "not try" is when they are totally exhausted, for example after a hard day of skiing. Remember the last time you really skied hard all day? You probably felt so tired that you could hardly walk; you were exhausted, but you were also relaxed. Fortunately, you don't have to exhaust yourself in order to not try.

Since you don't know how to not try, you should first try something you know how to do. Clearly, you know how to be tense. Simply tighten your muscles. For example, gently clench your teeth, then stop. When you let go of the tension, relaxation occurs. That is because by clenching the muscles you produce more tension than is common (or comfortable) for you, so it is easy to let go of some of it.

Identifying the Muscle Groups

Because there are many muscle groups in your body, you first need to identify them by tensing and relaxing them one at a time. Review the following process for identifying muscle groups. When you are prepared to learn them, set aside 15 minutes, sit back in a reclining chair or lie down on a bed and begin.

Hands and Arms Begin with the muscles in your hands and arms. To know which ones we are talking about, make a fist with your dominant hand as though you were gripping a ski pole, and cock your wrist away from your body. (For you tennis players, this is the same way you would cock your wrist for a forehand stroke.) Gradually tighten these muscles a little. There is no need to strain the muscles. You need only be aware of the tension produced in your fingers and thumb, the back of your hand, and your forearm. Now let go of the tension by unclenching those muscles. Do this as though you were suddenly dropping the ski pole or tennis racket from your hand. Notice that a slightly warm, pleasant feeling flows into your hand and forearm and that they feel slightly heavier.

The next set of muscles are those in your biceps. Gradually tense these by bending your arm at the elbow and curling your hand toward your shoulder. (This is the "Muscle Beach" pose.) To relax the muscles, drop your hand toward the floor. Notice the feeling of warmth that flows into these muscles and the heaviness that results.

Facial Muscles There are three groups of muscles in the face. The first is in the forehead and can be tensed by raising your eyebrows as high as possible so as to make horizontal frown lines across your forehead. The second group is around your eyes and cheeks. Tense these by gradually closing and squinting your eyes tightly. The third group is around your mouth and jaw. To tense these, gradually clench your teeth and purse your lips as though you were a baby stubbornly refusing to be fed dinner. Tense and let go of each muscle group separately so that you identify it and are aware of the contrast between feelings of tension and the warm, heavy feelings of relaxation that occur when you let go.

Neck There are two separate muscle groups here. You can tense the first by bowing your head and trying to force your chin gradually into your chest. Tensing the second group is achieved by gradually pushing your head backward against the back of the chair, a wall, or any other object that will provide resistance.

Shoulders, Chest, and Upper Back You can tense the muscles in these areas all at once. Do this by taking a deep breath and holding it in your upper chest. At the same time, gradually pull your shoulders back as though you were trying to bring your shoulder blades together. Notice that this creates tension in a band across your chest, around your shoulders, and across your upper back. When you let go of the tension in these muscles, allow your shoulders to slump forward as you let the air out of your lungs. Don't force the air out of your lungs; just let it go as you would with a deep sigh.

Stomach and Lower Back You tense the muscles in your stomach by taking in half a breath and gradually making your stomach hard, as though you were expecting someone to punch you there. At the same time, arch your lower back forward so that the small of your back is not touching the chair and you are sitting stiffly erect. Feel the tension—and let it go. Notice the contrast between tension and relaxation.

Hips and Buttocks Tighten the muscles in this area by gradually clenching your buttocks tightly together and tilting your pelvis forward so that the small of your back is touching the back of the chair. Then let go.

Thighs Clench the muscles in the front of your thighs by gradually straightening your legs and holding your feet off the floor. Let go of these muscles by letting your feet drop down with a thud.

Calves Point your toes downward to gradually tighten your calf muscles. It is easy to cramp these muscles, so be careful not to tighten them too much. Let go of the tension and allow the pleasant feelings of relaxation to spread into your calves.

Shins Along with your thighs, the shin muscles get the biggest workout when you ski. They are also the ones that are likely to be most tense during or after a day of skiing. Tense these muscles by pulling your feet upward and gradually pointing your toes toward your head, as though you were raising your ski tips just prior to getting off the chairlift. Then let go.

Feet These muscles can become cramped after a day of skiing if you have spent the whole day hanging on. When the muscles of your feet are tense, it is virtually impossible to get any flexibility in your ankles. You tense these muscles by gradually curling your toes downward and arching your feet slightly, as though you were trying to hang onto the slope with your toenails. Tense these muscles, notice the tension, and let it go.

The Training Program

Once you have identified each muscle group and are able to tense it and let go of the tension, you are ready to begin relaxation training. First you need to find a setting that is conducive to relaxation, some place where you will not be interrupted and where there are few distracting noises. Your body should be partially reclined and supported at the head, back, hips, legs, and feet. Reclining chairs are ideal but not essential. Stretching out on a couch or bed with your back and head slightly propped up will suffice. A comfortable easy chair and ottoman are also possibilities. Whatever furniture you use, you should be able to sit comfortably with your arms and legs uncrossed. The relaxation procedure works best with your eyes closed. However, until you are thoroughly familiar with the sequence of the various muscle groups, you may want to keep your eyes open so that you can refer to this book or a separate list.

Once you are settled comfortably, you are ready to begin the tension-relaxation process. For each muscle group, we want you to gradually tense the muscles for 5 to 7 seconds and then abruptly let go of all the tension by letting your muscles go slack. While you are tensing the muscles, focus your attention on the feelings in that particular muscle group. When you relax the muscles, be aware of the pleasant contrast between the feelings of tension and relaxation. Focus your attention on the feelings of warmth and heaviness that spread through each muscle group when you relax it. Allow that warmth to spread over your body and soak into your muscles. You should focus on the relaxation part for 15 seconds.

Initially this process works best if you tense and relax each muscle group twice before moving on to the next group. If you find that any muscle group is particularly difficult to relax, you may tense and relax it a third or fourth time. During this process you may find that your mind wanders. That's okay. If it does, simply refocus your attention to the feelings of tension and relaxation that you are creating in your body. Alternatively, you may find that you drift off so completely that you fall asleep, especially if you are doing this process at the end of the day. That's okay too. It is a sign that you are really letting go of the tension. If you find that you are repeatedly falling asleep during the relaxation process, however, you should try it a different time of the day and/or change your posture so that you are sitting in a more erect position. Let's review the whole training procedure:

1. Recline comfortably on a chair, couch, or bed with your arms and legs uncrossed.
2. Gradually tense each muscle group for 5 to 7 seconds, focusing on the sensations of tension in the muscles.
3. Abruptly let go of the tension and focus on the sensations of warmth, relaxation, and heaviness for 15 seconds.
4. Repeat processes 2 and 3 with one muscle group before going on to another.
5. When you have completed the tension-relaxation process for each muscle group in your body, take a few minutes to remain seated comfortably and soak up the feelings of relaxation throughout your body before you go on to any other activity.

The best way to learn this skill is to read the muscle group sequence into a tape recorder so you can play it back without having to think about what you are doing. Read the instructions for each muscle group twice, allowing 5 to 7 seconds during each instruction to execute the tension-relaxation cycle. Then allow 15 seconds of silence to experience the relaxation. For the first 2 or 3 weeks you should use the relaxation process at least once a day for 4 or 5 days a week. After this initial training you will find that you can relax each muscle group with only one tension-relaxation cycle and without the tape. Once you and your muscles become fully aware of the contrast in sensation between tension and relaxation, you will be able to let go of the tension in your muscles without tensing them first. You will also find that you can relax entire areas of your body at once, that is, you will be able to relax all the muscles in your face, legs, or hands and arms. Although you should practice this procedure in a private, quiet place, once it becomes natural you will find that you can voluntarily relax your muscles, genuinely letting go while working at your desk, driving your car, or riding the chairlift.

The Tension Check/Release

An important part of the relaxation skill is the ability to locate tension in your body. As you practice the relaxation exercises, you will become more sensitive to the presence of tension in specific muscle groups. Throughout the rest of this book we will be asking you to use this skill by doing a *tension check/release*. To do this you should focus your attention on the muscle groups in your body, one at a time, to determine the presence of any tension. If you notice that any muscle groups are tense, increase that tension slightly and let go.

Remember from our model of active awareness that kinesthesia allows you to sense your body. That is an important ability. As you gain experience in relaxation skills, the tension check/release becomes easier and you will be able to sense residual tension and let it go. And as you combine your relaxation skills with your skiing, you will be able to distinguish between normal skiing tension and anxiety-produced tension. You will be able to let the anxiety tension go almost reflexively every time you sense its presence. You have then developed an important skill: the natural use of cue-controlled relaxation as you are skiing.

Mental Relaxation

Tennis champion Yvonne Goolagong used to say when she lost concentration during a match that her mind went "walk-around." A meandering mind can wreak havoc with your best intentions, whether in tennis, skiing, or something as "simple" as relaxation. You may find that as you do your muscle-relaxation exercises, your mind is thinking of your job, a new pair of skis, or a fantastic party next Saturday night. Although some of these may be pleasant to contemplate, they do not facilitate relaxation. In fact, they may even cause you to tense up with eager anticipation or worry. This is especially true if your mind is buzzing from a day of strenuous or exciting mental activity.

Many solutions have been proposed for this problem. One approach advocates turning off your mind. But for many people that's easier said than done; besides, as we've said before, the mind is not an asset to be ignored. Instead of unplugging it, we have found that you can actually enhance your bodily and emotional relaxation by shifting your mental focus. Think of your mind as a receiving unit for a variety of electronic signals. Most of these signals activate you; they tighten you up with joy, excitement, anger, or anxiety. But a few of them calm you down. Those are the channels you need to select in order to enhance your relaxation. One of these channels is a visual one.

To experience this channel, go through your muscle-relaxation exercises until you are moderately relaxed. Then, with your eyes closed, create an image in your mind of a tranquil personal paradise. This may be a deserted tropical beach, a tall, silent mountain high above the timberline, a calm, grassy meadow near a babbling brook, or a fur rug in front of a glowing cabin fire. If none of these fit, make up your own. As you continue to let go of the tension in your muscles, transport yourself to your tranquil paradise. Allow yourself to float into the scene and settle comfortably amid your surroundings. Let go more and more. Whenever your mind wanders, switch the channel back to your paradise and sink into a state of relaxation.

Some people find that an auditory channel deepens their relaxation. You might play a tape in your head of a peaceful strain of music. If you are able to keep this in your mind without effort, great. Use it to complement your visual scene. However, other people find that the focused repetition of a simple sound is more relaxing. Sometimes the use of a single word is effective.

Choose a one-syllable word that has a neutral meaning or that denotes relaxation and sounds relaxing. A common neutral word is "one." Relaxing words are "calm," "warm," or "ease." Get into a comfortable posture and close your eyes. As you exhale, say your chosen word under your breath. At the same time, visualize the word (or the number "1"). When you inhale, don't focus on anything in particular; let your mind go wherever it chooses. As you exhale again, repeat the word to yourself. Repeat it with every exhaled breath for at least 5 minutes. Seven to 10 minutes is even better.

Another method of producing mental relaxation is an inner spatial focus. This is useful for deepening the relaxation you have already begun. To find this channel you need merely to initiate the relaxation process by letting go in your muscles or repeating a monosyllabic word. Then focus on the space between your eyes. Concentrate your mental energy on that space. If your mind wanders, switch the channel back to that space. As you increase your use of this procedure, anxiety will seem alien and will become a cue for you to relax immediately. While riding the chairlift or the subway, you will be able to let go of tension by tuning in to that space.

Negative Practice

Negative practice means exaggerating a behavior to its extreme limit and practicing that extreme. The tension/relaxation cycle is a mild version of it. In actual negative practice, you execute the behavior while skiing. It is useful both because it helps you increase your awareness of a problem ski behavior and because it helps you let go of it. Two images may be good examples of extreme exaggerations.

Remember when Dorothy first came upon the Scarecrow in "The Wizard of Oz"? After she got him to the ground, he was so loose and floppy that it took a while before he could coordinate his movements. In contrast, recall the Tin Man. He was so rusted and stiff that he could not move at all. True functional relaxation lies in between these two extremes. You want neither to be so relaxed that you flop around on the snow, or so tense that you can hardly move.

The objective in doing negative practice is to sensitize you to your tension levels by building mental and physical cues into your skiing. These cues let you know when you are too loose (i.e., on the front side of the performance/arousal curve) or too tense (on the back side of the curve). This is particularly valuable for detecting excess tension because you will be learning to use tension itself, detected at low levels, as the major cue to block further spiraling of that tension. In addition to helping you to monitor your tension levels while skiing, the following exercises also can be used as part of your morning warm-up routine.

Learning Negative Practice

Strangle a Pole Close your eyes, take a deep breath, slowly exhale. As you do, take a tension check by mentally examining your body for any excess tension and letting go of any you find. Hold your hands in your usual skiing position, poles off the snow. Gradually tighten your hands around your poles until you feel as if you're strangling them. Notice the tension in your hands and forearms. Maintain tension for 10 seconds. Let it go and hold your poles gently off the snow. Note the difference between tension and relaxation. Remember, it is the awareness of the difference that is critical rather than the absolute levels of tension or relaxation. Remain relaxed for 15 seconds. Repeat the cycle.

Breath Holds, Jaw Clamps, Knee Locks, Toe Curls These are analogous to pole strangling, only working with different muscle groups. Take a deep breath, hold it for 10 seconds, then let it out. Remain loose for 15 seconds. Gradually tighten your jaws till your teeth are clamped. Hold for 10 seconds, then release. Let your jaw hang loose for 15 seconds. Stiffen your knees until they are locked; hold, release. Hang loose, flexing your legs slightly, letting your boots support most of your weight. Curl your toes down in your boots; hold, release.

Repeat the entire cycle several times, or until you become aware of the characteristics of this type of tension. First work with one set of muscles at a time, then tense and relax all of them. Notice that when you are tensed up you're like the rusted Tin Man. When you release all that tension you are like the Scarecrow, all floppy and loose.

Ski Like the Tin Man, Ski Like the Scarecrow Before you push off, tense yourself up like the Tin Man. Make five turns as the Tin Man; hold your breath and remember to lock your knees. Then with a big sigh, let go of your breath and all that tension. Become the floppy, loose Scarecrow and make five more turns. Notice any differences in your skiing? Repeat the entire sequence, but this time, after the five Scarecrow turns, make five more with a little more energy. By now you should be finding the most appropriate level of tension for this slope.

Using Negative Practice

Negative practice is a powerful tool, and in fact it often is the most efficient route to handling tension on the mountain. Assuming you have learned and practiced your tension-relaxation cycles, you are able to identify excess tension quite clearly. Although toes curling downward may not describe you, and you may not have a problem with excess tension in your hands, each of us does have habits similar to these. It may be stiffening a downhill leg, tensing your quadriceps (thighs) as you sit too far back, or tensing your neck as you stiffly maintain your gaze 2 feet in front of your skis. Now do the following:

1. Become aware of your tension cues as you are skiing.
2. Choose one that is clear and (at least in the beginning) located in a smaller muscle system such as your hands or toes.
3. Each time you pause in your skiing, take advantage of that time for negative practice of your inappropriate tension. Greatly tense the muscle system, experience the tension, and then let go a moment or two after you experience it.
4. As you succeed with these, move to larger muscle groups.

In practicing this process you will discover that the presence of your tension as you ski cues you and almost *causes* you to let it go and ski more relaxed. Remember that it is not a one-shot operation; it must be practiced in order to become a part of your skiing habits. If you let this happen you will be pleasantly surprised by your accelerated progress.

Exercises

1. Practice the physical and mental relaxation exercises at home until you can let go without first tensing your muscles.
2. While reading, riding in a car, or working at your desk, focus your awareness on your body. Let go of any extra tension that you notice. Do the same while riding the chair lift.

Exercises to be Done on Snow

1. Practice momentarily letting go of the tension in your whole body between turns, especially in conditions such as bumps or ice that usually cause you to tense.
2. Use the feeling of speed as a cue to drop your hands, loosen your grip, press forward slightly, and relax.
3. Use negative practice for persistent feelings of tension.

Often when we get caught up in the excitement of skiing, we forget much of what we are trying to work on and we end up just "going for it." Sometimes that's okay, if we are *ready* for this. But being ready means sensing that our bodies are relaxed enough to be at the peak of the performance/arousal curve. If we are not ready, we may get so caught up in our emotions that relaxing is the furthest thing from our minds. And yet it is precisely at these times that we need to relax the most. One way to remember to pause and relax is to use the surroundings as visual cues to do a tension check/release.

The next time you get to the top of a beautiful run, take a minute to look around. Notice the grandeur of the scene, the tree line, the blue of the sky, the way the light filters through the trees. See it as a restful, relaxing picture. At the same time, do a quick tension check and release. At first you will have to make a conscious effort to do this, so make it part of your routine of preparing for a run or while riding the lift. With enough repetition, each time you see the tree tops or the sky or the sunlight filtering through the trees, you will find yourself beginning to let go of excess tension.

CHAPTER 6

Mental Imagery and Mental Rehearsal

The power of mental imagery should not be underestimated; some athletes can tell you why. Consider Pirmin Zurbriggen, the Swiss winner of two golds and a silver at the 1985 Alpine Skiing World Championships in Italy. About 3 weeks prior to his triple medal performance, he injured the cartilage in his left knee in a World Cup downhill. He underwent arthroscopic surgery. Anticipating the Championships, he began to exercise his knee—and his mind—within the day. He watched videotapes of his races, mentally rehearsing them over and over again. He said to the press, "I raced while I was in bed, and that's why I didn't lose the feel for it" (*Sports Illustrated*, Feb. 18, 1985, pp. 18-19).

If you were among the millions of television viewers who saw Phil Mahre just before his gold medal run in the 1984 Olympics, you saw him with his eyes closed, hand snaking through imaginary gates, mentally skiing them.

Debbie Armstrong, on the night before her Olympic victory, attended the pairs figure skating awards ceremony. As she watched, she imagined herself up on the podium. She later related to the press, "I tried to memorize that scene in my mind, and visualize it was me standing up there. I went to bed with that image in mind."

If there is one common theme in the writing and research on sport psychology, it is that of the power of mental imagery. Chapters 2 and 3 illustrated mental imagery as it relates to fear and to self-punishment. You may have noticed with some concern that your process of imagining may be getting you in trouble. By beginning with two chapters that deal with some of the things we all mentally do wrong, we chose to take advantage of what seems a common emphasis on the negative. That is, as psychologists and ski instructors, we have heard repeatedly the distressingly common question from students, "Tell me what I'm doing wrong!" Clearly, the mental rehearsal of what you are doing wrong, what you are anxious about, or what you are upset about is not in your best interest. As will become clear over the next chapters, we prefer to concentrate on what to do right. However, by starting with what you are doing wrong, we hope we left you with a strong and personal impression of the power of your mind. Now let us turn to some general thoughts on mental imagery and mental rehearsal and introduce you to their considerable power in the *positive* direction.

The Various Images of Imagery

"Visualization" is a term commonly referring to mental imagery. Although it may be one facet of imagery, it is perhaps a misnomer because of its narrow meaning. If you have ever taken an advanced skiing or racing workshop, perhaps you have been led to the top of a difficult run where the instructor gave directions like, "I'm going to ski about 50 yards. Watch me carefully. When I stop, close your eyes, visualize yourself skiing the same way I did, then open your eyes, and ski." But people differ in the way they visualize, and you may not be able to see anything in your mind.

If you are like some skiers we have met, when asked to close your eyes and visualize, you expect to see a nice picture of yourself skiing like a pro. But all you get is black, punctuated with some afterimages and colored dots! However, the problem may not be with you. Instead it may be the narrowness of the term "visualization." Its literal meaning implies only seeing. Yet, just as you experience skiing through all of your senses, you may experience visualizing through senses other than (or in addition to) seeing. For example, you may include awareness of muscle movement and pressures, emotional feelings of competence or frustration, and possibly hearing.

Here is an example of an interaction of these modalities as you automatically perform a sensory transformation from visual to auditory to kinesthetic. Read and imagine the following:

The other day we were in a classroom and the instructor scratched his fingernail slowly down the blackboard.

If you cringed when you created that mental image, you know what we mean. Imagery in each of the senses will vary along three dimensions. Imagine yourself a racer, visualizing in a complex combination of senses. You see the gate ahead. You are flying into a very tight turn, hearing your skis chatter on a rutted and icy course. You are aware of the vibration in your feet and legs as the pressure on your thighs builds quickly. Even in such a complex image, there are three dimensions of imagery that apply: point of observation, intensity, and control.

Point of Observation

From where do you visualize yourself? Reminding yourself that visualization includes all of the modalities, do you see yourself as a TV camera would? That is, are you outside of your own skin, seeing the powder fly up around you and billow behind you? Or do you see an untouched, crystalline blanket of white ahead of you, the tips of your skis occasionally rising above the snow? How about in the bumps? Do you see your knees bending, absorbing and responding on each turn, again as a TV camera would? Or do you *feel* your knees bending, your thighs absorbing and flexing as you reach out to the next turn?

As you can guess, it is more likely you will be using your kinesthetic sense if your point of observation is from the inside. In other words, you will be feeling your limbs, your musculature, your state of tension/relaxation, and your balance. By contrast, it is more likely that you will be using your visual sense if your point of observation is from the outside.

Although the research is not clear as to which is the more helpful way to visualize, we do know that an important part of visualizing is getting your nerves and muscles to imitate your skiing movements. It is our position that visualizing from the inside is a skill worth acquiring in that it most accurately reproduces what happens when you are actually on your skis. (When you are just learning to ski, of course, you do not yet know how it should feel. At that stage of the game, simply seeing from either point of view is helpful.)

Intensity

Many years ago it was demonstrated that as one imagines a muscular movement (for example, striking a nail with a hammer), there is a measurable electrical response in that muscle. Recent research suggests there is a positive relationship between intensity of imagery and physiological responding. Intensity can be defined as the vividness or focus of your imagery. For example, imagine a very specific skiing scene such as a giant slalom course set with red and blue gates snaking down a hill. You might see that scene clearly, in sharp focus. Or the same scene might be an image that is less intense, the gates ill defined and without color.

From our perspective in sport, the more intense and focused our mental imagery, the more benefits we reap from the process. Although it will take some practice, we have found that learning to intensify your imagery is well worth the effort.

Control

This refers to the degree to which you actively control the definition and continuity of your imagery. Mental rehearsal must include a clear definition of the specific skiing situation you are trying to work with and the goal you wish to achieve. The necessity of clear definition of goals was discussed in chapter 4 ("Active Awareness") and should be reviewed if you are uncertain about it. If for example you are mentally rehearsing some difficult gates in a course, the sequence of those gates—and what you wish to accomplish as you ski them— must be carefully defined.

You must also control the movement of the imagery so that it has continuity, flowing as do real-life events, from beginning to end. A "still shot" image, like a photograph capturing you as you graze by one of the difficult gates, is not as effective as well controlled continuity of your image. You do not actually ski from pose to pose, nor does your activity stop midturn. Mental rehearsal reflects real life. This means that in the racing example you must imagine skiing *through* the tough spots on the course.

Learning Mental Imagery

There is a wide variation in our ability to create mental imagery. Some of us are able to create vivid *visual* images, others are able to more easily create *emotional* images (by actually experiencing through imagination strong emotions such as fear, jealousy, or joy), and still others are best able to create *kinesthetic* imagery (images of feeling our bodies in space and motion). At this point, you may wish to take stock of your ability to create imagery in each of these modalities. Although there is no meaningful test we can offer you in the pages of a book to make that judgment, you might wish to jump ahead to Appendix C on "Learning Mental Imagery" and familiarize yourself with how we suggest you go about learning or enhancing your ability to create mental imagery. If it does not seem to fit, continue now with the following section on how to use imagery to enhance your skiing; if it does fit, please do take time to do the suggested exercises. Your investment will be well worth it.

Using Mental Rehearsal

Someone got the idea to go to the moon. With no experience being in moon orbit prior to separation of the lunar lander and no experience rocketing off the moon's surface to get back to the ship to go home, we somehow ended up with "One small step for a man, one giant leap for mankind." And we did it without landing on the moon for a practice session. There is a lesson here, and it can be applied to our ski psychology.

Certain uses of mental rehearsal emphasize the programming of your neuromuscular responses so that your body comes to "know" what to do in specific situations. Other uses emphasize dealing with emotions, or anticipating and solving problems. Just as training the astronauts to get to the moon was accomplished by programming responses to complex situations and by rehearsing problem-solving skills, so too can your skiing be helped by simulating and rehearsing skiing (and thinking) skills. The three major uses of mental rehearsal are as follows:

1. To "wire-in" neuromuscular responses involved in the skiing activity or skiing problem you are working on;
2. To deal with emotional components of your skiing or ski competition by centering your arousal on your performance/arousal curve; this includes decreasing your arousal by using relaxation imagery and by "inoculating" yourself against problems that could occur and lead to poor performance. It also includes increasing your arousal by psyching up;
3. To increase motivation by rehearsing a dream.

Wiring-in Neuromuscular Responses

This is probably the most common use of mental rehearsal. In order to begin wiring-in, you and your body need to know something about the appearance and sensations of the activity. This knowledge grows from the preceding exercises through which you developed kinesthetic awareness and increased your ability to create and control imagery.

Wiring-in the Past When you use mental rehearsal to wire-in the past, you use yourself as your model because you are mentally rehearsing your own past performance. That could be the five turns you just finished, that bump run last week, or that field of bottomless powder last year. If you use yourself as your model, you are probably satisfied with your performance. If you are not, you should move ahead to other techniques such as using others as your model.

Your imagery should be as intense and well defined as possible. Your point of observation is optional. The continuity may be limited to five turns in the middle of the run or three gates in the middle of the course. Within those turns or those gates, however, the image should be flowing. That is, it should not be a still photo of yourself.

As with all mental rehearsal tactics, wiring-in the past is not a one-shot operation. It takes discipline—but only a moment—to pause at the end of each series of well executed turns to recreate them. The image you rehearse may be an emotional high, a finely tuned kinesthetic image, even a detailed visual image, or (ideally) a combination of these.

There are two immediate benefits to wiring-in the past. First, it is a rewarding and motivating experience. Second, it provides a wealth of material for future mental rehearsal scenes.

Wiring-in the Present Wiring-in the present requires others as models. It is an ideal way to start if you are not yet comfortable with your own skiing, and it is especially well suited to getting the most out of a ski lesson. It is also useful for expert skiers and competitors trying to bring their skiing up to the performance of another expert. It is a form of learning by looking, which we will cover in detail in chapter 7 on vicarious learning, but it has an additional goal of programming a neuromuscular response until it becomes reflexive.

To wire-in the present, watch your model (maybe your instructor) with body English. To watch with body English requires you to slightly move your own muscles in synchrony with the model (as you will learn in chapter 7). You then close your eyes and continue the scene in your imagination, rehearsing *yourself* doing what you have just seen. We suggested that you do this as you were developing kinesthetic awareness and imagery. Its continued use goes beyond these goals as you increasingly wire-in what is presently happening. Like wiring-in the past, the present provides valuable material for future imagery scripts.

Wiring-in the Future This is often called previsualization. When you previsualize, you are drawing upon the mental imagery scripts that you have previously wired in. It is previsualization that is most commonly mentioned by the newspapers and TV. Recall, for example, the attention on Phil Mahre as he mentally ran his race, moving his hand through imaginary gates.

To use previsualization, you must have your imagery script well defined. This presumes a good level of active awareness. It also requires discipline; you can be no more satisfied with previsualization as a one-shot operation than you can be satisfied with one good turn on a bump run. Rarely should you push off to ski without previsualizing where you are about to go and what you are about to do. Only with this kind of consistency will you learn to accurately compare your actual skiing movements and your intended movements. Additionally, previsualization of skiing a course through the bumps before you actually do it will help you get into your peak state of physiological/psychological arousal, and it will help you memorize the terrain.

Incorporate all of your senses and be sure to mentally rehearse the entire distance you intend to ski. We recall a college racer who would often slow down or lose it at the finish, regardless of what went on earlier in the course. We knew she used mental rehearsal and previsualization, so we asked her to relate her imagery to us as she experienced it. After several such sessions we realized that she never told us she was imagining herself finishing a race. When asked about this, she said she did not think it was necessary because her previsualization was so realistic and it felt so right the way she was doing it. No wonder she had trouble finishing races. Through negligence, she had rehearsed *not* finishing hundreds of times! The simple tactic of having her include *finishing* her races in her mental rehearsal seemed to help a great deal, since she soon began to finish with more consistency and with better times.

You may occasionally wish to solve a specific problem with mental rehearsal. In that case, previsualization is helpful only if you have successfully overcome the problem at least once in the past and have wired it in, or if you have a good model, instructor, or coach who can provide material for mental rehearsal through demonstration or verbal description. If you have this material you may begin attacking the problem a step at a time. Once you get your foot in the door, accomplishing to your satisfaction a part of your goal, you may begin using yourself as your model and your previsualization will be far more efficient.

Previsualization can be used at home, riding to the area, on the lift, or during dull conferences. Make a boring moment useful! It is often a fine time to use mental rehearsal. You can enhance it by incorporating your immediate environment into your fantasy. A breeze becomes the wind in your face. A pencil becomes a pole. Your shoes become your boots.

A young friend of ours, an excellent ballet skier and aspiring all-around freestylist, was bringing home some rather poor grades. His parents were justifiably proud of his skiing but perturbed about his academic performance. His teachers felt the same way. They inquired whether the young man was daydreaming about skiing. Sure enough, he was, but what they considered daydreaming was his mental rehearsal. He was rehearsing his art. Although the grade issue remains unresolved, his freestyle is improving dramatically!

Centering Your Arousal

Emotions are bipolar—there are two ends to every emotional scale. Consider the more general emotional state of *arousal*. That too is bipolar. In skiing, and especially in ski competition, it is possible to be either too aroused or not aroused enough. Consider the performance/arousal curve and you will recall that either side slopes off into less than optimum performance. Fortunately, there are mental rehearsal strategies you can use on either side of the curve. If you slide off one side or the other of the curve, then you should be using these strategies to center your arousal.

Increasing Arousal   Often in skiing alone or practicing for an upcoming competition, there is too little arousal. In other words, there is a need to psych up. Increasing your arousal requires that you work with your emotional imagery. To do that you must have learned several mental rehearsal scripts that are arousing. Examples would be the sounds of spectators at your last race, the recollection of your friends watching you and then complimenting you, and the sensation of standing at the top of a perfect run anticipating your turns.

The approaches to psyching up usually involve recreating your scripts of past performances and/or past audiences. One of the oldest experimental demonstrations in psychology showed that simply being observed enhances performance. For those among us who are not elite racers, the recollection and rehearsal of skiing with friends, imagining them with you, is a good tool. For you elite skiers, imagining your competition as well as your audience would generally be more useful.

Decreasing Arousal A much larger problem is that of too much arousal. Usually when performances suffer it is due to a lack of concentration and a racing mind, or too much muscular tension. Remember that muscles work in opposition to one another. That tense tricep behind your arm pulling against the tense bicep on the front of your arm is going to result in an absence of movement in any direction.

All sport psychology programs with which we are familiar include training in deep muscle relaxation and training in quieting the mind. Since it is such an important skill to learn and rehearse, we covered that separately in chapter 5. If you are aware that you are too aroused at the top of a run—either because of fear, anger, or even being too eager—that is the time for mentally rehearsing your relaxation skills. Please remember, however, that unless you have practiced the skills, they certainly will not be available to you when you are attempting to back down from very high arousal levels!

But how about actually practicing dealing with stress *before* you get to your starting gate? This is called "stress inoculation" and it is enormously useful. Stress inoculation involves mentally exposing yourself to the stress in gradually increasing doses and then mentally rehearsing the correct response to the stress. You begin with little doses, just as vaccines are given in doses designed to be too low to hurt but strong enough to build up an immune response.

Stress inoculation accomplishes several things. First, it offers an opportunity to rehearse the problems before they come up. Second, it adds to your repertoire of problem-solving tools. Third, your arousal to new, nerve-racking events is vastly decreased (the sounds of a large crowd, taunting by competitors, unusual environmental occurrences, etc.). Using this mental rehearsal technique requires the following:

1. You must know relaxation skills.
2. You must know in some detail what are your stressors.
3. You must be able to experience the anxiety associated with that stressor by creating and guiding your emotional imagery.

4. You must know what skills you need to accomplish your goal (e.g., changing your self-talk, hitting a gate differently, or looking at a bump run differently).

Get as relaxed as possible and then use your stressors in your imagination to create emotional imagery. You will use that imagery to gradually increase the intensity of the emotion that you are feeling as you learn, in the safety of your mind, to apply the required coping skills. Here is an example of a young student of ours applying stress inoculation to the anxiety-producing taunts of competitors:

Charlie had been upset on several occasions by competitors on his racing circuit. His competition was made up of senior high students in various school systems across the state. Because he tended to lose his temper and shout in response to the taunts of fellow racers, the taunts became meaner and more real. He began to tighten up, got increasingly angry, and his times began to suffer. It was clear that he was on the wrong side of the performance/arousal curve.

We asked Charlie to become aware of when he began to feel angry and get tense. He said it began as people were gathering around the starting area but before the actual taunting began. It got worse as people would make teasing comments. It was worst when he was in the racer-ready position. At that point any small yell would cause tension. We jotted down a few of the teasing comments that would shake him up.

We then asked him to come up with some comments he could use to tell them he could take it. He suggested several: "I'm going to look at those gates, not listen to them." "I'm going to relax and go for it." "They can tease me at the bottom after they see my time, if they still want to." "Just relax. They'll stop after a while, and I've got a hot race to run."

We then asked Charlie to set aside 15 minutes each night for 3 weeks or so to think about and hear in his mind the taunts of his competitors. When his emotional imagery made him feel tense, he was to take a breath and calmly make one of those remarks to himself, repeating it until he began to relax and could imagine himself doing well on the course. We asked him to turn up the volume on his emotional imagery as he got better at resisting the teasing in his mind.

He happened to be a good student about this; spending a few minutes practicing each night, he felt better after a week or so. His times were improving in 2 or 3 weeks, which helped him feel even better. Finally, the teasing stopped when his taunters were not getting any more reaction.

If you wish to use stress inoculation to center your arousal, you will have to make at least as much of a commitment as Charlie did. Not too much to ask, but definitely requiring some dedication. You may have to include self-talk in your imagery, as did Charlie, or certain skiing skills such as rehearsing a quiet grip on your poles. If your problem is something like fear of riding a chairlift, you would also have to include some basic relaxation skills, along with changing your self-talk about the "dangers" of chairlifts.

Rehearsing Your Dream

It is a superhuman task to become an Olympian. It takes an energy and commitment that is difficult for many of us to understand. The discipline, the practice, and the relentless pressure often seem to go unrewarded. The competitions may start at age 5 or 6. The struggle is punctuated by spectacular highs and horrible lows, by victorious moments shared with closest supporters and defeats often faced alone. In their struggle the athletes must move past those friends who have fallen by the wayside, and they must transcend the nagging conviction that the only other person who might truly understand the loneliness is another athlete. But the most extraordinary thing about this struggle is the fuel that energizes it. That fuel is a dream.

It is dreamt as one endures the pain of pressing mental and physical skills to the absolute limit, only to realize there must be another limit, and then still another. It is dreamt when one watches a competitor who is turning in a superb performance. It is dreamt as one rests after an intense practice, exquisitely in tune with body and mind. And it is dreamt, as Debbie Armstrong did, when one witnesses a victory celebration. Although we are not all Olympians, we all need a dream. Your dream is motivational, it offers an ideal image of yourself, and it can be very helpful on rough days.

A dream differs from other mental rehearsal techniques. It is powerful in its own way. It is different because it is a flowing big picture, a reverie more global than the small parts of your skiing added together and analyzed. It is thus a "gestalt," a whole that is greater than the sum of its parts.

Dreams also differ from other mental rehearsal techniques because they are more emotional. Your dream includes emotion as a central theme. By contrast, you could pick apart your skiing and your ski psychology bit by bit and not generate emotion. Even though recreating your emotions is probably necessary in order to use several of the other psychological techniques in this book (for example, stress inoculation or assessment of your position on the performance/arousal curve), dreaming creates a more powerful emotional experience and feels as if it is doing so more naturally.

Dreams differ on a third and final point: They are uniformly positive. If they are not, you should absolutely not be rehearsing them. (For bad dreams, you will be using the earlier material on stress inoculation, and the material on constructive thinking that you will learn in chapter 9.)

Rehearsing your dream to improve your skiing means that you must have the kind of dream we are talking about. It is an experience we all share, that of losing oneself in a daydream. There are two cautions here: First, keep your dreams positive. Second, be sure you are dreaming of yourself. Strangely, dreaming of yourself is not as obvious as it sounds. We have met people who dream of other skiers in an "I wish..." format, firmly lodging the other skier in their mind. To work, your dream must be about you.

Dreaming Out of Rough Days

From time to time the going does get rough. Whether we ski for recreation or competition, we all have bad days on the mountain. Sometimes it seems impossible to ski yourself out of it, problem-solve yourself out of it, or talk yourself out of it. The characteristics of a dream work for you on such days. Instead of trying to bull your way through it, you could use something that is nonjudgmental and from your heart instead of your mind. On rough days most of us over-analyze and our minds race with "shoulda's and oughta's." A dream on a day like this offers the big picture—the gestalt we referred to earlier—so that your racing mind slows down.

Using your dream on rough days is different from using imagery for wiring-in your skiing or for solving problems. Recall that specific problem-solving with mental rehearsal is judgmental, evaluative, and involves dissecting the problem. We are not suggesting that dreaming supplant other types of mental rehearsal. But we are saying that you should learn to be actively aware of those days when you cannot seem to stop being your own worst enemy—of those days when your picking apart a problem is getting you nowhere. On such days then, by all means, let go, smile, and settle back with your dream.

Dreaming for Motivation

Like the carrot on a stick, a dream motivates. You can look outside yourself or inside yourself for a motivating dream. There is always a better skier/model on the mountain, and as you are gaining skill in your skiing that person becomes more than just a stimulus for mental rehearsal of kinesthetic awareness. He or she takes on meaning that is more akin to a concept of skiing. It is as if you are feeling *with* the skier far more than just the sum of the parts of his or her skiing. Your dream then becomes the big picture of you, with all of its wholeness and emotion and idealism.

Look outward for these models and the concepts they represent. One such concept is of a flowing, top-to-bottom bump run. Another is the concept of winning. We guess that as Debbie Armstrong was experiencing the ice skating awards ceremony, she was feeling an emotional, holistic sensation. We would guess that it was far more than the parts, such as the music or the crowd or the smiles. All of the training endured over the years culminates with those awards, and that is realized in one's guts, not one's analytic self.

Look inward for that skier in your mind. It is especially helpful when, coincidentally dressed and appearing as yourself, that skier is skiing as your ideal self. Your dream *is* your ideal self. Unlike mental rehearsal for specific problem-solving, for example, it is a nonjudgmental, generous, and caring view of yourself.

Because it is an ideal image, your dream of yourself is not a basis for negative comparison or self-criticism. It is safe and it is especially inspirational. If you think about it for a moment, there are not many examples of how we psychologically use *ourselves* as our own inspiration. Even as we attempt to avoid being our own worst enemy, that attempt does not usually extend to generosity with ourselves. But a dream! That is safe, warm, private, and emotionally supportive—and certainly greater than the sum of our parts.

View your dream as if it were the thread in a necklace. It is the thread on which to hang your precious peak experiences. Your successes are strung together. When things are not happening for you, you know that you are in one of the blank spaces, but still on the thread. To rehearse your dream at these times is to push ahead to the next gem.

Use your dream on the chairlift. Drift off to sleep at night with your dream. Let yourself be lost in your reverie as you sit in the whirlpool after an energetic day. Let it be you on the mountain, or on your own victory pedestal.

Beyond Imagery

There are many tactics to change your skiing and ski psychology that are not imagery techniques. Their emphasis is to change your ski behaviors more directly, and to do so *before* you change the way you think. This direct approach has two benefits. First, certain skiing habits actually invite problem imagery, as you learned in chapters 2 and 3 and will learn further in forthcoming chapters. In that case, we will suggest the road to minimizing problem imagery is by working directly on those habits. Second, any specific habit changes you make that lead to rewarding, competent skiing gives valuable information to your mind and to your body. That information, and the good skiing experiences you are having, provide outstanding material for future mental rehearsal. We turn now to some of those direct techniques.

Vicarious Learning: Learning by Looking

Mark, a college racer, had begun skiing only 4 years before attending college. During high school he lived in an urban area far from snow and had little exposure to skiing. Yet, in his first year of college he became the best technical skier on the team. After a year of seasoning with college competitions, he became a good racer who placed well in most races. Prior to his coaching in college, he had never had any formal instruction.

Have you ever wondered why some skiers improve so rapidly with so little instruction and practice? "Oh, they're just natural athletes," you say. Perhaps, but as we explained before, skiing is not a natural sport. It challenges our instincts for balance and self-preservation. Yet some are able to overcome all of these natural hazards and learn to ski relatively quickly. As Mark's coach (W.C.L.) observed,

When I first saw Mark ski, I asked him how he had learned so quickly. I expected him to say that he had spent several winters in the mountains. Instead, he replied that he skied *only on weekends. He'd made friends with some good skiers who took him to Mammoth Mountain. "Well, did they give you a lot of instruction?" I asked. "No, nothing much beyond what equipment to buy and how to put it on. We were a quiet bunch, and we didn't talk much when we were together. They just skied, and I watched and did what they did." Taking Mark's experience with his friends as a key to how he learned best, I coached him primarily by having him follow me, first just in free-skiing and later in practice runs on race courses. His progress was astonishing and gratifying. By the end of the year he was technically one of the best skiers on the team.*

Mark's rapid improvement is a classic demonstration of what psychologists call "vicarious learning," or "modeling." Modeling is not new to psychology or skiing. Psychologists have used this principle to help people over their paralyzing fear of snakes, heights, crowds, and public speaking. Ski instructors have also used this principle. When they say "Watch me!" and carve smooth turns down a steep slope, they are not doing it to show off. The ski instructors are demonstrating the right technique for their students. And modeling is one of the best ways to do it. Almost anything that can be learned directly can be learned vicariously, that is, by watching someone else do it and then practicing it yourself. As you will read in Appendix C on mental imagery, to use visualization effectively it is useful to have a model to visualize.

Qualified Modeling

There is one major qualification concerning the effectiveness of vicarious learning. For vicarious learning to have a positive effect on your skiing, you need to be relaxed, alert, and at least neutral in your self-talk. If you are angrily discounting your ability to ski well or to stay relaxed, you will not be able to use the model. You are neither focused nor relaxed enough to mentally rehearse and absorb the image of that skier. Because your emotional state interferes, you may conclude that you cannot do it, are no good, and will never get better. As you now know, that kind of conclusion makes you your own worst enemy, further aggravates the problem, and becomes a self-fulfilling prophecy.

Availability of Models

Not all of your vicarious learning about skiing comes from ski instructors or other good skiers. Although an instructor has shown you the best technique, many other people on the mountain are showing you how to stiffen your downhill leg, stem every turn when you're trying to ski parallel, or bounce off the bumps when you should be absorbing them with your knees. The errors skiers make are far more obvious than the subtleties involved in truly fine skiing. They are also easier to identify with because the response to loss of equilibrium is universal, natural, and well within the observer's experience. Weight distribution shifting slightly, subtle edge changes, independent leg action, a hint of tension here and relaxation there—all of these are much more difficult to read than a flailing pole, a stiffened body, or an edge left unset. Actually, you already know how to do many of the incorrect things. As we showed you earlier, your body will naturally do those things in the interest of self-preservation. What you learn vicariously from the poorer skiers is to be anxious and stiff when you should be relaxed and self-confident.

An example of this is the common tendency to stop at the edge of steeper terrain. Recall the last time you approached the steepest part of a run. First, you stopped at the top to peer over the edge. You can always tell that a difficult section of the trail lies ahead because a lot of skiers are stopped at the top of it. Wondering why everyone had stopped at the top, you watched a few others start down and you focused on the skiers who were having the most difficulty. Their skis were slipping rather than edging, their legs were locked in one position, their arms were stiff and awkward. In short, they looked petrified! While you watched, your body also began to stiffen. You felt the way they looked. That was vicarious learning. So when you pushed off down that pitch, you skied it with the same awkwardness they did even though you are a much better skier!

You may also have observed some skiers who handled the difficult slope with ease. If you focused your mind on them and imitated their relaxation and good technique, congratulations. You used vicarious learning to your advantage. However, we have found that most people manage to cancel out the positive modeling provided by the better skiers on the mountain by saying something like "Gosh, they're good. I can't imagine skiing like that." If that's you talking, there goes your own worst enemy again. That is indeed unfortunate, for it is precisely your imagining you *can* ski like that which is the essence of vicarious learning.

You can make modeling work for you or against you. Either way, it will affect your skiing. This is especially true of your emotional responses. By observing relaxed skiers, you can facilitate relaxation; by observing skiers staying in the fall line, you can decrease your tendency to traverse too much. And by observing skiers who are having trouble, you can bring back all the fear and tension you thought you had conquered in the previous chapters!

The Unconscious Model

One of the main requirements for modeling is that the observer identify with the model. The stronger the identification the stronger the learning, other things being equal. If you have a very strong identification with someone, you may unconsciously copy his or her behavior.

Several seasons ago we were asked by the coach of a small college ski team to help him solve a problem with his team's performance. It seemed that the entire team was in a slump; specifically, they were having trouble finishing courses. They would start out late, and only the two or three best athletes were able to catch up. Most of the others would eventually blow out of the course. Dave, the coach, believed that the problem derived from a lack of readiness in the starting gate, but no matter how much he emphasized getting psyched at the start, the problem kept returning.

After a morning of indoor rehearsal and some on-snow work on relaxation and visualization, we asked Dave to set a slalom course.

"Do you have anything special you want us to do?" he asked.

"Yes, we do. Just run a regular practice as close to race conditions as you can make it. We'll watch and see if we can detect anything that might give us a clue."

Dave entered the start, continuing to give directions and words of advice. He did not appear to be concentrating on the course. At the "racer ready" signal, he began to turn his attention to it, and at "go" he pushed off. He skied the first two gates nonchalantly, not really getting into a rhythm until the third gate. Then he skied smoothly and powerfully to the bottom.

Next in the gate was Mel, who, according to Dave, was the best slalom racer on the team. At the "racer ready" signal, Mel appeared distracted. He fidgeted with his poles and looked off to the side of the hill. At the count he seemed to pull himself together, and at "go" he pushed off. To our surprise, he skied the first two gates just as Dave did, rather nonchalantly, getting later and later in his turns until it was only by a tremendous effort on his part that he was able to stay in the course. But he had to give up so much speed that there was no way he could have made good time.

Jill followed Mel, and—you guessed it. She too skied the first gates with almost no intensity, got late, and had to give up too much speed to make the third gate. It was not until she passed the second gate that she seemed to get any power into her skiing.

Racer after racer repeated the pattern, with many blowing out of the course. At first we thought it was a joke. But no, they were not aware of the source of their problem. They were all modeling Dave!

Dave was apparently unaware of his lazy starts and that they had been imitated by his team. All the skiers would ski the first two gates lazily, waiting until the third gate before they would put some intensity into their skiing. By then it was too late for most of them; they could not catch up. The solution was clear. Since there was no video available to show him how he was skiing, we decided to help Dave become aware of how his own skiing was influencing his team. We asked him to change the way he was running the course because it was influencing the way his team was performing. We suggested that Dave imagine himself in a race each time he ran a course, and to start off as aggressively as possible and not be concerned with falling.

We also had each racer previsualize skiing the first two gates before they actually ran the course, building their feelings of energy to a peak to coincide with the "go" signal. In *this way, upon leaving the start they could burst out with a surge that would carry them through the first two gates.*

The change was dramatic. With Dave leading the way, it was not long before the entire team was charging out of the start. Some problems still persisted, of course, but they were less a result of starting slowly than of not being used to starting aggressively.

When you watch someone ski, you will be modeling some part of that person's skiing whether or not you are aware of it. So be careful who you watch, especially in a lesson. Don't simply model the person who went in front of you. Make sure you keep your instructor in mind.

The Tense Model

At a national downhill training camp one winter, the coaches showed a film of a very difficult downhill racecourse the night before the actual race. The film showed racer after racer rocketing through a bumpy section of the course at 60 miles per hour, losing control and crashing in an explosion of arms, legs, and skis. The tension in the room was incredible. Any fear that had been conquered while practicing for the race was resurrected by the experience of watching the film. In the race the next day, those competitors who had used their minds to control their anxiety skied well. Those who hadn't were left to the same fate as the racers in the film. Many good skiers were in the latter group.

That should be a lesson in itself. *Don't watch tense skiers.* The racers in the training camp should have focused on the skiers in the film who did not fall. Tense skiers have nothing useful to teach you. You don't need them to show you how steep the slope is, how hard the ice is, or how heavy the powder is. Your body will reflexively tell you if the terrain is difficult for you. You need to let your body relax.

The Talking Model

Remember how you can be your own worst enemy by making self-defeating statements? Your friends can be your enemies as well. Recall the last time you were skiing with a friend on a difficult slope. You were both trying to do your best; you were handling it well but your friend was really having trouble. She or he said, "Damn it all. This is really tough. I can't ski this stuff. I'm just not having any fun." The farther you skied, the more your friend complained. Maybe you empathized with your friend. After all, you know what it's like to be having a bad day. So you agreed, "Yeah, this is tough stuff," and you began to ski less aggressively. Soon, instead of your skiing the mountain you discovered that it was skiing you. And you began making the same self-statements your friend did. "Damn it all. I can't ski this stuff anymore. This isn't any fun."

The lesson here is simple: *Don't listen to a skier who is having trouble.* If your friend is being his or her own worst enemy, don't let that person become your enemy, too. In chapter 14 we discuss how to help the minds of your friends. To do that, you first need to use your own mind. So for now just don't listen when other skiers complain. If necessary, ski alone for a while. The adage "Hear no evil, see no evil, speak no evil" makes a lot of sense when applied to your skiing! This does not mean you should turn off all your senses when you ski. The emphasis in the adage is on "evil," meaning tension, fear, and self-defeating statements. We want you to use your powers of observation to your advantage, not to your detriment.

The Fashion Model

Since "looking hot" is a goal for many skiers, you may be tempted to imitate the flashiest-looking skier on the mountain. Don't. What looks flashy may be the worst thing for your technique. World Cup champion Ingemar Stenmark is one of the least flashy-looking skiers in the history of ski racing. When he races, he rarely looks fast to the untrained eye. Yet he is one of the best. He does not look fast because he does not waste any motion. On the other hand, there are many flashy skiers with a lot of excess motion. When you learn vicariously, you imitate the most obvious elements. Unfortunately, the most obvious elements in flashy skiers are frequently the least essential.

Picking Your Model

To use vicarious learning to improve your technique (the physical aspects of your skiing), pick a smooth, steady skier to imitate. A smooth skier is modeling relaxation and balance, not speed or extraneous motion. Unless you want to be a racer or a freestyle competitor, don't pick a racer or a hot-dogger. This is not to say that racers and freestylers are not good skiers. They are. It is just that they may not be the best models for what you want to achieve. A ski instructor is usually one of the best models you can find. Short of that, choose a friend who skis the way you would like to ski. Watch him or her. Just look. That sounds simple enough but it is not.

Most of us cannot just look. We have to look with judgment. To demonstrate what we mean, recall the last time you watched a skier whom you wanted to emulate. What were you thinking? You might have thought something like, "That skier is terrific! I wish I could do that." You watched by judging. A better way to look is by experiencing what you are seeing. If the model is floating through loose powder, feel *your* body floating. If the model is absorbing the moguls, feel yourself absorbing the moguls. Practice looking without judging in the following exercise:

Turn on the television but not the sound. Simply observe, without comment, the actions of the people on the screen. Relax as completely as possible, letting go of tension, and then experience the movements of the people. Try picking out separate actions if that seems easier at first. Then, put it back together. Let yourself experience the whole person, the whole action. Do this several times, or until you feel you are genuinely experiencing, without comment, your TV model. You should finally be able to experience all or just part of the model simply by tuning in without comment whenever you wish.

Once you know how to look, you should know what to look at. That all depends on those aspects of your skiing you identified as needing change. Look at that aspect of the model that relates to your objective. The following are examples of things you may have slated for change and the corresponding aspect of the model that you might watch and experience vicariously. You should ask your ski instructor for examples that are more specifically tailored to your skiing.

Problem	*You might watch and experience*
• Moguls	Legs flexing and extending
• Weight too far back	Fanny; hands at end of turn
• Powder	Up-and-down motion of whole body
• Ice	Angle of knees into hill; edge control
• Tightness	Knees; whole body flowing from turn to turn

Imagine yourself actually experiencing the movement you are watching. Recreate that feeling when you ski. We discussed this in chapter 6 on mental rehearsal. If you have difficulty visualizing the gestalt, review that material.

Body English: Active Observing

We want you to go one step further than passively watching and feeling that you are in the model's body. You will learn to imitate the model's movements more effectively if you move your body in concert with the model's while you are watching. Physiologically you are teaching your nerve fibers a new set of responses and you are integrating those responses with what you see (visualization) and feel (kinesthesia). The more repetition there is of those nerve responses, the more you wire-in those movements. Moving your body while you are watching is similar to the body English that golfers exhibit while watching the trajectories of their shots, as if to influence the ball to stay out of the woods. Although their movements have no more influence on those trajectories than your movements would on the model's line of descent, you will be teaching your body some useful skills while watching. And hopefully, your models can stay out of the woods on their own.

Warming up With Modeling

Pretend you are at the mountain, about to begin a day of skiing. When you begin your first run, what do you usually do? Most skiers think about which run would be the easiest warm-up run, the greatest challenge, or the least crowded. If you are aware of your body not being loose, you may do a few stretching exercises before you push off, but you probably do not do anything to get your mind and body together.

One of the best exercises we know for getting your mind ready to ski is observing someone who skis well. Before you start your first run, perhaps while you are still on the lift, watch. All you need is a good skier who is within view. As you watch, experience the sensations of that skier's movements. Actually put yourself in that skier's body. Before you push off on the first run, feel the movements that your model makes. We have found that doing this *consistently* at the beginning of the day significantly decreases the time most skiers take to get their minds and bodies working together.

The Contagion of Joy

Thus far we have been talking about how to use modeling to learn physical technique. As you know, modeling also applies to your emotional learning. If other skiers look scared on a certain slope and you pay attention to them, you will feel scared. And you will ski scared down that same slope. On the other hand, you can ski joyfully if you have a few joyful models around. Several classic laboratory research studies demonstrate this phenomenon, and it can be used to your advantage.

Laughter and joy are contagious. So is courage. If one of your problems is that you become afraid, discouraged, or depressed, it helps to be around someone who is happy and unafraid. When you observe the model's joy or fearlessness, let yourself experience it. And be careful not to discount the model's emotions by telling yourself, "Well, she's only feeling good because she's skiing well. If I could ski like that, I'd feel great, too." It is equally likely that she is skiing well because of the way she is thinking and feeling.

Have you ever noticed a group of people skiing together and really enjoying themselves? It does not matter whether one of them is falling all over the place. The skier is still having a good time because he or she is participating in the joy of the group, learning the positive emotions of skiing through his or her companions. The person is using the group to psych up, and it does not cost a penny extra. You can do the same.

The Contagion of Film

There is another place where the vicarious learning of good skiing can occur: at the movies. We are not saying this just to promote ski movies. The fact is, contemporary skiing films present images of skiing that we typically do not have an opportunity to observe. Powder is an example. Rarely can we just stand and watch turn after turn executed by a fine skier in champagne powder. Either we are not in a position to do so, or the unspoiled expanse ahead of us is beyond our self-control and we are in it too! Cinematographers also go to great lengths to show us long sequences of skiing, often using helicopters, multiple camera placements, and zoom shots that our eyes are not capable of. Our eyes and our bodies just cannot make it around the mountain like that. Finally, slow-motion sequences can show aspects of skiing that we might never otherwise observe.

Using film as a learning tool is not much different than using live models. The same considerations apply. You should be nonjudgmental, allowing the image to be absorbed without evaluative comment. You should be relaxed. You should (ideally) know what you are looking for, although film is enjoyable and probably still useful without this precision. Finally, you should take every opportunity to watch with body English, getting "into the skin" of the model with kinesthetic awareness. So watch the film, experience the flow of the skiing, and let your imagination soar.

Modeling Reminders

The next time you go skiing, identify an aspect of your skiing that you would like to improve. It can be something physical like having looser knees or a more centered body position. Or it may be something emotional like feeling more joy or self-confidence. Be aware of the possible models to imitate. At first it may even help to do an active-awareness analysis of their skiing. Once you have selected and observed a model (without judgment on your part), imagine yourself in the model's body and experience his or her movement or emotion. Create that experience for yourself as you watch. Then take the experience with you when you start down the mountain.

Enhancing Performance With Operant Techniques

Meet Dexter M., IV: Dexter, being a fourth-generation M., was a proud soul. He was a fine tennis player, a competitive business person, and a hard-driving, beautiful skier. At least under certain conditions he was a beautiful skier. Under other conditions he was neither a beautiful skier nor a beautiful person. (He was, however, always proud, competitive and hard-driving.) His nemesis was a steep run with bumps. When he encountered this terrain, his beauty disappeared and he fell apart. And the more he fell apart, the more he pushed and failed. The more he pushed and failed, the more he harassed himself. His private monologues centered on his inability to make a series of smoothly linked turns on those conditions. Instead he made a series of roughly linked recoveries. Each bump would throw him farther back; he would stiffen, swear, stiffen some more, recover, swear—and continue pushing, proudly and with utter frustration, from top to bottom. "Since my hard-driving approach works well in business, why shouldn't it in skiing?" he wondered.

"Okay," he finally said to himself, "I'll take it one step at a time, probe with some active awareness, and change this idiocy." He did exactly that. He focused on the problem, felt his body stiffen while his head was spinning with self-punishment, and was able to pinpoint his difficulty. Specifically, he always began his series of recoveries after the first two or three bumps and just kept on pushing.

At this point he began to inquire about his contexts. What preceded this problem? Only sharp, steep bumps. He would stop at the top of the pitch, contemplate the bumps, grit his teeth with determination, and go. The first few would cause automatic efforts to regain his balance. That hint of stiffening in turn brought on the punishment and self-statement to keep pushing: "I can, I will, I am going to do this if it kills me, keep going, keep going...." This was followed by an increased determination to push harder on the next run. And the cycle would begin again.

Several tactics in *Skiing Out of Your Mind* zero in on problems similar to Dexter's, or like the fear problems others of you might experience. They are based on the principles of operant learning that point out that your skiing, both the good and the bad, is not an accident. You learned it; it is being cued by certain conditions and maintained by certain payoffs, but the psychology can be changed.

Since the operant learning of skiing is voluntary, you can bring it under control by doing one or both of two things: (1) Change antecedents, that is, those contexts that cue you to ski and think in a certain way. You can do this by changing your exposure to those cues or by changing the value of the cue. (2) Change consequences, that is, change the payoffs you get for skiing as you do. This can be approached by eliminating the payoffs entirely or by increasing the payoffs for better skiing habits in conjunction with decreasing payoffs that maintain your own personal embarrassments.

It would be so gratifying if skiing were a straightforward matter of learning the physical skills required. Then you could just take lessons and "go for it." Your head would never get in the way. Your payoffs would be that those physical skills would always work to let you turn with grace, float exquisitely through the powder, and flow like mercury through the bumps. Each of you would ski your fantasies. Instead, we see errors that are universal. We see stiff legs, tightly clenched poles, and awkward falls. We see skiers who are out of control coming to a stop with relief, and skiers standing on top of steep pitches contemplating disaster rather than joy. These are the obvious errors. We also see fine skiers, the experts, getting angry with themselves and seemingly unable to master that anger.

These are all places where operant psychological strategies help. You *can* control the antecedents and consequences of your behaviors and thereby improve your performance. The strategies are straightforward and immensely helpful—*if* they are used systematically and consistently. If they are not used consistently, the price you pay is frustration and an *increase* in the power and persistence of your nonconstructive bad habits. On the other hand, if you are consistent and systematic, the positive changes in your skiing are going to surprise even the most optimistic among you. Put another way, the cost-benefit ratio is very much in your favor.

Controlling Your Antecedents: Interrupting Problem Triggers

Let us turn first to the control of antecedents. You can consistently change your exposure to the personal contexts that control your head and your skiing. Here is an example of an almost universal tendency of skiers to let the mountain ski them:

The Lookers

Imagine yourself skiing along a trail, perhaps one that is familiar to you. You know that there is a steep pitch, a rather sudden change in terrain ahead. You arrive at that spot. Recreate that scene right now. What do you do next? What is going on around you? If you are like most skiers, you stop! You join several people contemplating the pitch ahead, perhaps overhearing a comment or two about the bumps or the skiers halfway down. You have let the mountain ski you, and in doing so you have made a cardinal, though easily changed, error: *You stopped at precisely the wrong time.* Like other errors in skiing, the stopping was natural. It was predictable, especially among beginning and intermediate skiers. You have probably been speeding up on the easier terrain that preceded it, and it is natural to slow down because of a change in your environment. You are sensing an anxiety-arousing event *before you encounter it.*

There are problems with this seemingly innocuous habit. First, you have lost whatever rhythm and forward motion you had. Second, as you are standing there mulling over the pitch ahead, you have plenty of time to be your own worst enemy. Listen to yourself. What are you saying? Is it self-generated fear-talk? Whatever it is, you are likely to be mentally rehearsing the worst. Third, you may be observing some skiers on the way down ahead of you. Let's suppose they are struggling. What are you rehearsing about how they must feel? Or suppose the skier is good, executing her turns beautifully, pointing her skis down the fall line and really flowing. What are you rehearsing to yourself then? Is it something like "I wish I could do that!" or "Damn, she's good!"? Perhaps you even make some such remark to another skier standing a few feet away.

You must stop psyching yourself out and control your anxiety arousal. How does operant learning relate to that? Simple. *Control your antecedents. Don't stop at the crest of a steep section.* Slow down, perhaps, if it is a blind pitch, but retain your movement and rhythm. The antecedent that you discover during your active-awareness analysis is the terrain change. You were under what is called *stimulus control* when you stopped. The pitch, the moguls, and the people all "conspired" to trigger your worst-enemy dialogues, your involuntary emotional arousal, and your observational learning.

So, one thing Dexter did whenever possible was not to stop at the top of a steep pitch. His wasn't a problem of fear but rather that the pitch cued a determination, a gritting of his teeth, a tension throughout his body that set him up for being thrown back in the bumps. This of course would trigger even more tension. By not stopping, he began to break the cycle by giving himself less opportunity to grit his teeth.

Let's take a moment to dismiss a couple of replies skiers have made to these suggestions. First: "I stop because I'm tired when I get there." If you know that the pitch is coming and feel you will be too tired to continue when you get there, stop 100 yards above it and rest. Then reestablish your rhythm, relax, and ski over the crest. Second: "I *have* to stop on steep hills." If you feel you must stop when skiing the steep, do it after you have rhythmically skied a hundred feet or so over the crest. You can certainly psych yourself out there, too, but it is somewhat less likely—particularly if your first several turns were good. Besides, it quickly becomes rewarding to ski right past all the lookers at the top of the pitch!

How much more straightforward could a tactic be? It requires only the systematic alteration of a voluntary natural habit. Now you are beginning to ski the mountain.

The Stoppers: From Weakness to Rhythm

Here is another natural error that skiers make, one that is also found among very fine skiers and can be corrected by a simple operant-learning strategy. Imagine for a moment that you are skiing one of your favorite hills. You have nice rhythm and are executing some delicious turns. All of a sudden you catch an edge and lose your balance, which results in a reflexive tensing of your muscles. Now, recreate that incident. What do you do next? Imagine that sequence, and imagine what happens then.

If you are like most skiers, you stop! You think back on the close call: "Damn, that was close, must have caught an edge." Or you slam your pole against the snow in frustration: "I'm awful." And so forth. Though your script may be slightly different, you are making the behavioral error of stopping at precisely the time you should be regaining your balance and rhythm. Just as stopping at the top of a hill puts you under stimulus control, so does this error (a natural response) set you up for inappropriate mental rehearsal. It is an antecedent that invites catastrophizing, and it teaches you nothing. Even the best skiers sometimes lose control, of course, but it is the beginning and intermediate skiers who are most likely to come to a full stop. It is an error that invites the self-generation of fear (and anger, too, if you are feeling frustrated), an error that you can least afford to make at that point.

But there is another, equally damaging result. Learning to regain control is just not possible when you stop from a position of weakness. The solution to the problem is as straightforward as in the previous case. Control your exposure to the antecedent events. *Simply do not stop.* Regain your balance. Relax. Let it flow. Slow down, perhaps, especially if you were out of control. But above all, flow into a couple more turns. If you are thinking you are tired at that point, go ahead and stop—*but not until you stop from a position of strength, a position of balance and control.*

Shaping Better Skiing

There are as many different types of cues controlling skiers' habits and minds as there are skiers themselves. Although you now know, through the process of active awareness, how to pick out those stimulus cues (antecedent conditions) that specifically affect your skiing, it often is difficult to change your exposure to them. For example, if you want to learn to ski powder but it precipitates your feeling tense and telling yourself "I don't know how to ski this," you are seemingly caught in a bind. If you try to ski it while you are stiff and tense, you are likely to fall or to stiffen reflexively to avoid falling (and thereby increase the probability of falling anyway!). Even if you do not fall, you will have learned to ski powder stiffly and awkwardly. Either way, skiing in powder has become unpleasant. And because you (and we) naturally avoid unpleasant situations, you are likely to avoid powder conditions. Recall that all it takes is a few pairings of loss of balance and certain ski conditions to cause your avoidance responses to become automatic. On the other hand, if you avoid it, nothing new can be learned. The problem here is that you have gotten yourself into an all-or-nothing situation. Either you take deep powder all in one gulp ("face-plant," to be exact) or you have nothing to do with it. The solution is to take it in moderation.

The best way to learn to ski powder is to take a powder lesson, but here is an example of a shaping progression that has worked for many of our students in all but deep powder or heavy "cement." On a powder day, before it has been packed, find a slope you know and are comfortable with. The powder should not be more than 5 or 6 inches deep.

Begin by making a short run in as steep a traverse as you dare, and come to a stop by turning uphill without crossing the fall line. Do this to both sides, gradually increasing the steepness of your traverses until you can start off straight down the hill and turn out of the fall line to a stop. When you can do that comfortably, add a smooth flexing of your legs through the turn so that they are fully flexed when you stop. Extend your legs, start into the fall line again, and repeat to the other side.

Next, instead of coming to a complete stop, extend your legs before you lose your momentum and start a turn in the other direction. This is the part of powder skiing that gives people the most trouble. The resistance of the snow makes the turn feel different than on a packed surface, and many new powder skiers try to force their skis around into the new turn. But if you have been practicing turning out of the fall line you know that you can do that without forcing the turn, so you can now let your skis go into the fall line with just a little effort on your part. Once they are there, it's easy to complete the turn just as you have been doing, and you're on your way. Whenever you get a chance, practice some more and gradually work up to deeper powder.

Sneak up on it. That is the most efficient way to describe shaping techniques. Shaping means successive approximations, taking a step at a time. In so doing, you are gradually changing your payoffs while simultaneously changing the value of the contexts that cue your problems. Shaping is effective in both areas because it involves a relearning and reperceiving of the situation.

Managing Traversing Troubles by Shaping

Skiers share a number of avoidance behaviors that could be easily modified by systematically taking things a step at a time. The keys here are "systematically" and "a step at a time." The classic examples are the beginning or intermediate skiers as they traverse back and forth across a hill, afraid to make that first turn down the fall line. All of this traversing is not an efficient way to learn to ski. Admittedly it is a normal avoidance response, that is, a skiing habit they have taught themselves in order to avoid excess speed and imagined speed-related catastrophes, like going face-first into a tree. The problem is that it becomes a habit, a nonthinking behavior.

We could draw upon any number of illustrations of this, but the most extreme case was that of a young man who would ski across difficult slopes, slow down, sometimes stop, and stiffly step around to begin his next traverse across the hill. At least he was skiing the advanced runs, he thought. He was also chopping up the run, much to the chagrin of the advanced skiers sharing the space with him. Most skiers with difficulty in speed control find themselves skiing across the hill in a manner far less exaggerated than this young man, but nevertheless progressing slowly if at all.

If this type of problem characterizes your skiing, this is how you could apply *shaping*: Find a section of the hill that is easy for you. Visualize a path, perhaps 15 feet wide, going straight down the fall line. Ski it, making a few turns. What you are trying to do is change your psychology. You are beginning to shape a new skiing behavior. It is important that you start with a hill that is easy for you. Remember that you have learned the traversing problem because of your original reflexive response to loss of equilibrium. You have learned that traversing works to save you most, if not all, of the time. So you are not learning anything new. That is why you must begin shaping strategies with easy tasks. The last thing you want to do is relearn your avoidance responses or learn new ones. You do not want to stay tense or anxious—an easily observable characteristic of traversers.

Set your standards realistically at first. Achieving a realistic goal will enable you to tell yourself, "Well done," and will help dissolve fear. You will be demonstrating to yourself that you can ski the hill without losing control. You can now do one of two things: You can either progressively narrow the trail so that you force yourself to make more frequent turns, or you can move to a slightly steeper part of the mountain.

If you are a more advanced skier, the same strategy is useful. Picking a trail through the bumps and skiing it is difficult at first. The shaping approach to this problem requires the same graduated success experiences as for the beginner or intermediate skier. You might stay on the steeper, bumpy hill and get off two turns, then three, then four, and so forth. Or you might pick a trail through the bumps on a somewhat easier run and practice it consistently before you move on to something steeper. You will be learning to pick a trail and almost photograph it in your mind. And as you begin the run, if your first turn is good the chances are that subsequent turns will be good.

Skiing "Bad" Snow

Wet, fresh snow is a problem for many skiers. It becomes a problem for most skiers when it gets chopped up. We have observed skier after skier avoid the sides of runs after fresh snow because it has been chopped up rather than skied down (as in the center of the run). Shaping tactics are useful here. The question is, how might "bad" snow be approached within the guidelines thus far discussed? You may think the answer is to stand in the bad snow, make just a few turns under control on a reasonably easy hill, proceed with a few more linked turns, and then move up to progressively steeper hills. That sounds logical, but there is a better way.

In all cases of shaping, you must try to take advantage of skiing skills you already possess. It makes better sense to get your rhythm established where it is reasonably unchopped, and then proceed into the chopped area for a few turns and then out again. Begin, perhaps, with one turn in and out. A criticism of this strategy is that it is harder to make the transition from relatively smooth skiing into irregular snow, so why make it more difficult? The observation is correct but the conclusion is not. If you do an active-awareness analysis of the situation, you will realize that the inconsistency (change) in the snow condition is the same one that has triggered your avoidance in the past! You never stay in it long enough to learn it. Perhaps you get thrown off balance in the transition, ski out of it, and stop with a few thoughts like "Whew, got to stay out of that stuff!" We have seen this happen again and again. You are teaching yourself the *difficulty* of that ski condition. Also, the transition into "crud" from smooth snow requires unpredictable changes in weight distribution and edge control—exactly the skill required when you are skiing chopped snow. So start from a position of rhythm and stability, ski into the crud, and accomplish those things at the same time.

Since the technique of shaping is not particularly difficult to use, it seems strange that so many skiing problems persist. Though "shaping" is in fact a technical term for a type of psychological intervention that is used frequently with clinical populations, one hardly needs to be trained in psychology to understand it. Why, then, do so many personal embarrassments persist in the face of trying with so much effort to be rid of them?

Problems may persist because these four shaping guidelines were not followed:

1. Be gradual. Take your time. If the problem is big enough to work on, we suspect you have had it for a while, so do not expect it to disappear at first try. You need some success experiences or you surely will give up the effort. Whether you are an outstanding skier or a beginner, many personal challenges remain for you. Understand that we are *not* saying do not challenge yourself. We are saying *do not resensitize* yourself.

2. Set your goals realistically. You could be sensible in the type of run you work on but unrealistic in the time you set to achieve your goal. As you are now aware, standard-setting is often a major psychological problem for skiers. You simply set yourself up for failure, predictably fail, and thus confirm your self-critical judgments.

3. Be consistent and systematic in your effort. This point is crucial. Suppose you attempt to shape new ski behaviors only on those days when you say to yourself, "Oh, yeah, I remember that chapter. I think I'll *Ski Out of My Mind* for a few runs and try that shaping stuff." Then you do it, quit for lunch, and return to banging down the hills in the way that is typically you. What price do you pay? You will resensitize yourself and ingrain your bad habits even further. And what are you saying to yourself at the same time? Are you angry with yourself? Are you disappointed this chapter did not work?

4. If you do not have the physical skills required, get some tips on technique from a certified instructor. Many times, however, our experience has been that skiers do know what is required and what they are doing incorrectly. They just cannot seem to change. In that case, shaping tactics are especially helpful.

Low-Probability Skiing

If you have ever said to yourself, "I turn better right than left," you have engaged in low-probability ski behaviors, that is, behaviors that occur less frequently than you would like. All skiers share this problem. Since you turn better in one direction, you stop to the side that favors your strong turn. You are practicing your strength, which doesn't need it, while ignoring your weakness, which does need practice. The payoff of course is avoidance of instability.

The psychology is easy to change. After identifying low-probability ski behaviors—all those circumstances in your skiing of which you can say, "I do it better this way than that"—systematically shape new ones. Let each occurrence be a cue to change your low-probability habits next time.

Here are a few examples of what we mean.

Your "Weak-Side" Turns

If you turn best to the right, give up your search for a right-handed mountain. Instead, start on the *right* side, that is, your *strong* side, of most runs. This forces you to turn left with the same frequency that you turn right—or suffer consequences such as going into the trees. Doing this prevents you from slowly sneaking your way across the hill, toward your strong side, as you descend the mountain. Have you ever noticed how many skiers start on the side of a run corresponding to their weak side and end up on the opposite side? They are not completing their turns to their weak side because it would feel too unstable. The payoff for emphasizing their strong side is the avoidance of that feeling of relative instability.

Your "Weak-Side" Stops

You probably favor one side over the other for stopping. In other words, when you initiate a stop you initiate to your strong side. Change that. Let each intention to stop become a cue for using your weak side. By "cue" we mean a reminder to yourself to stop to the other side. You will be surprised at how quickly you can balance your stops.

Path Pounding

Change your psychology so as not to be a path pounder. In other words, always try to take a fresh track down a run. If you did it down the center and loved it, great. Now use that psychological momentum to explore something new. On the next run, stay 50 feet to the left. On the run after that, try the right side of the trail, and so forth. Two benefits accrue. First, you get more variety of terrain and experience. Second, if you had a bad run the first time, you've gotten away from the cues that were associated with it. If you have another bad run 50 feet away, it's still okay. At least you did not wire-in that one track. (Did you ever wonder why your skiing ended up in a rut?)

To sum up, use some active awareness to find out whether you have low-probability quirks in your skiing. If so, let that be a cue to consciously choose and increase the low-probability behavior rather than avoid it. You will then be working on what needs the most practice.

Reward New Skiing Strategies

The major reward for skiing well is the feeling of balance, rhythm, and stability: feeling your edges set, flowing over and around the moguls, getting airborne and coming down well, executing nicely rounded turns. These skills provide the joys, the exhilaration of skiing. They help quiet fear, anger, and self-criticism. The point is this: The reward for new skiing techniques largely depends upon whether the techniques work for you, not whether someone rewards you for them. "Working" is, of course, a personal definition that takes us right back to goal-setting. If you set your goals unrealistically high, many strategies you attempt will be doomed to failure before you begin.

Rewarding new skiing strategies is therefore a question of rewarding yourself for meeting personal challenges. As you consistently use shaping tactics to meet your goals, you will have a unique experience in skiing. If you are like many skiers, you will meet more challenges with more success than you have in any similar time span until now. You will be punishing yourself less, and you will be improving more. Most important, you will be enjoying *yourself* more as your own skiing companion.

And so Dexter slowed down. He decided to map out a shaping approach to solve his problems. He knew the technical skills required, and proceeded to take things one step at a time. On somewhat easier hills he picked a trail and began skiing it, flowing with it. He stopped from a position of balance from time to time, and then continued. He moved to some steeper hills, still consistent and systematic in his use of shaping, and things began to flow together even more beautifully. He also realized he was now getting his money's worth for the price of a lift ticket.

No magic at all. Simply active awareness and consistency in his quest for smoothness, with the help of some operant learning principles.

Reminders

1. Recreate several instances in which you have avoided certain terrain or ski conditions. Now, note whether there were discrepancies between your avoidance responses and your "I wish..." or "if only..." comments. This recollection will be used to help identify areas you wish you could change but have not thus far worked on constructively.
2. Again recall your conscious decisions to avoid certain terrain or conditions. Do an active-awareness analysis of your internal and external environments. Conclude the exercise by designing a realistic and gradual shaping approach to the problem.
3. Itemize those times the mountain is skiing you. Do you stop at the crest of pitches, for example? Formulate a plan to change your exposure to those cues, using a shaping process.

CHAPTER 9

Constructive Thinking: Changing Your Self-Talk

Recall the material in chapter 3 on being your own worst enemy. If you are like a lot of skiers we know, you were having some conversations *with* yourself *about* yourself (and your skiing) as you read that material. Our experience has been that it hits most skiers right between the eyes.

The fact is, however, you cannot just stop talking to yourself. You have been having these monologues since childhood. You may have observed that young children talk out loud to themselves while playing. That activity decreases as they grow older; the stream of conversation becomes internal, but it continues unabated.

"Right," you say, "I'll just change my self-talk from fear or anger to constructive advice." For example:

I'm not going to be angry. I'll concentrate instead on what I should be doing. Don't be so stiff! Mogul threw me. Don't sit back so far. C'mon, self, reach out with that pole. Don't let your arm get behind you like that. Pulls me back. Relax that leg. Don't face uphill!

Sad to say, this tactic will not work either. A stream of what-not-to-do's will set up a reemergence of the anger (or fear) talk. This chapter explains what *to do* in order to change your self-talk from being a hindrance to a help.

Differences Among Skiers

We have asked many skiers of all levels of ability what is going through their minds at various times on the mountain. We have found differences among them, both in frequency and theme.

Advanced skiers and fast learners seem to have an overall lower frequency of destructive private monologues. Their self-talk is more of a help than a hindrance. They are challenging and coping more. Beginners, many intermediates, and slow learners seem to have an overall higher frequency of damaging monologues. Their self-talk is more of a hindrance than a help.

Themes also vary. Beginning and intermediate skiers seem to have more of a problem with fear-talk. Beginners are in a strange environment with strange new sensations. If you are a beginner, the feeling of long boards clamped to your feet, perversely waxed to make them go faster, is strange indeed. Beginning/intermediate skiers are skiing new runs, perhaps wanting to push harder, but talking to themselves about the vagaries of moguls. You may swear that moguls actually reproduce themselves there in the light of day. Certainly they must grow in the dark of a moonless night!

For advanced intermediates and beginning experts, the self-talk tends to center on themes of frustration, anger, and impatience. Truly expert skiers also tend to get angry with themselves, but their destructive monologues occur much less often. They have learned to psych themselves up instead of out, setting personal goals, seeing the run as a challenge and the bumps as exhilarating, feeling their bodies and their skis. As an example, when we asked many expert skiers what they were thinking at the top of a very difficult run, we found it was almost invariably something like, "I'm picking out the best line down," "I'm challenging myself," "I can't wait."

Another common response was that they were feeling themselves skiing it, or practicing in their mind (the subject of chapter 6, "Mental Imagery and Mental Rehearsal"). They certainly were not thinking, "I wonder if I can do this" or "This run always kills me."

Mastery Versus Coping

We can roughly distinguish two ways of dealing with problems: mastery and coping. In the mastery model, the objective is to make the problem disappear. Theoretically, anxiety is reduced to zero, negative thoughts cease to exist, anger is completely supplanted by reasoned objectivity. You are supposed to master your work, brought up to believe that hard work will be justly rewarded. The hard-driving behavior so characteristic of us as we scurry about trying harder to master our environment is a response to the high expectations we Americans have: promotions, good grades, perfect kids, a higher standard of living. This is similar to the "Type A" behavior pattern that has been correlated with increases in heart disease, stress, and even sexual problems.

Well, "trying harder" does not work for sex, and it does not work for skiing. Apparently it only works for Avis. The problem with the Type A approach is that it invites an almost constant stream of self-criticism and tension, a preoccupation with the *product* rather than the process. Yet, like many other paradoxes in skiing, it too is "natural." Pushing has always been heavily reinforced in our society, and there is no reason to believe we skiers are less susceptible to social learning than anyone else is.

The coping model, on the other hand, demands no miracles. Its emphasis is on *process* and *progress* rather than product. The product will come. You will flow, relax, float, and ski in harmony with the terrain when you focus on the process of your skiing and attend to the progress you are making toward your goals. Your goals can be reached, but why do it the hard way?

Learning does not happen instantly. You can enjoy progress a step at a time. It all depends upon whether you perceive through a mastery model, which demands perfection, or a coping model, which allows for progress. You crashed miserably in deep snow...or you fell laughingly in the fluff. You complain that there were five skiers ahead cutting up a trackless bowl...or delight that you were the sixth, rejoicing in a crystalline day. The glass is half-empty...or the glass is half-full. As the humanist psychologist Clyde Reid puts it, "Celebrate the temporary." Relax, enjoy, experience the freshness in each new turn, the faces in the lift line, the sound of your skis, the squeak of the snow.

It is probably impossible to eliminate judgmental and evaluative self-talk in skiing. Your body reflexively tenses when you almost fall. Your mind reads that as "I must be afraid. My body is tense." That is the natural part of skiing and, of course, the reason your body is rather ineffective at teaching itself to ski.

But in coping, you can relabel. You can see and interpret the problem in a slightly different way. You can begin to modify your private monologues and use more accurate or appropriate interpretations of your skiing or ski conditions. In many cases this amounts to self-instructional training of the sort in which you are instructing yourself to take things a step at a time, relax, and so forth. Here are a few examples:

- Watching an instructor and imitating poorly, you say, "I'll never learn this!" The more accurate interpretation would be, "This is difficult at first, but I'm learning."
- As an advanced intermediate on a moderately steep run, you say, "If I can't ski this by now, I ought to quit. Why can't I stay relaxed?" Alternatively, you could say, "Stop. Take a couple of deep breaths and relax. Okay, let's flow over these next several bumps. Good! That felt much better."
- As an expert skier falling in the bumps, you say, "Dumb! You'd think I'd have learned by now!" The appropriate interpretation is something like, "I really had my rhythm. I just sat back too far. I need to keep reaching forward on my pole plant."

When we guide people in modifying their self-talk, they tend to voice a common reaction: "It is hard to believe this will help." Privately they are saying, "I can say it, but I don't think

I believe it! It won't make me feel or do better." Try to avoid the pitfall of talking yourself into a failure experience. The facts are these: first, you *do* generate a great deal of emotional arousal by talking to yourself; second, your physiology *does not* really distinguish between internal and external input; and third, you *do* define yourself and your skiing by the way you talk to yourself about it.

Your S.E.L.F.

To help you change your private monologues from a hindrance to a help, we developed a four-step process. It follows the acronym, S.E.L.F. In practice, these flow together and are not so discrete.

1. Stop. Stop your thoughts of fear, anger, and catastrophizing. They have done you no good and will continue to be useless.
2. Evaluate. Evaluate your standards. What do you really expect? Are you setting yourself up for failure by expecting too much too soon?
3. Label. Label what happened realistically. Reinterpret what happened using a coping statement.
4. Follow up. Follow up with reinforcing comments. Be good to yourself; compliment yourself for accepting and meeting your personal challenges.

S.E.L.F. Modification of Your Fear Monologues

Recall the equation, *risk minus fear equals peak experience.* If you are a skier with a fear problem, you probably recognize that much of it is self-generated. You are psyching yourself out (thinking how fearful you are) by letting the mountain psych you out (for example, stopping at the top of steep pitches). We acknowledge that risk is present, but the fact that you are skiing means you apparently wish to take some risk. You now need to subtract the fear.

Stop Your Thoughts There are several ways to do this. Distraction is one; for example, concentrate on the sound of your skis. What psychologists call "thought-stopping" is another. It works like this: First, get in touch with the contexts under which you begin your fear-talk. The common contexts are: after falling, while stopped above a steeper pitch, and when your body is already reflexively tense. Next, vividly imagine and recreate one of your fear-producing contexts. Establish the scene in your mind, feeling the anxiety, experiencing the context. Then abruptly slap your hands together, yelling "STOP!" (and we do mean yelling, right from the gut). This action will almost certainly stop your imagination and vivid feeling of the scene. Practice it several times with different scenes. Then begin to phase out the hand slapping and yelling and, instead, "yell" it under your breath. Practice this technique several times a day for a week.

You are now ready to use it on the mountain. When the fear monologues begin, yell "STOP!" in your mind. By so doing, you are initiating change in your self-talk by decreasing the perseverance of your catastrophizing. Stopping your thoughts is an essential first step, but it needs to be supplemented by the following steps.

Evaluate Your Expectations Almost simultaneously with thought-stopping, you should ask yourself, "What did I expect?" Serious injury? A huge catastrophe? You should be able to arrive at a clear definition of your fear. Of what *exactly* are you afraid? What clearly is the most disastrous thing that could happen? Precisely how will you hurt yourself? If you have not done this type of analysis, do it now. You will need to develop this ability enough to be able to do it on the mountain. You may be surprised to find that when defined and carried to their logical conclusion, many fears are blatantly irrational. Others need more work.

Label You have attached destructive labels to your tension ("I'm terrified"), to your falls ("I almost killed myself"), to the hill ("This is tough"), to the light ("I can't see the bumps. I'm going to crash for sure"), to the snow ("I can't ski this"), and so forth. If you do have a problem with apprehension when you ski, and if you are honest with yourself, you can at this moment recreate some of those monologues. The process of using more appropriate labels is also called "countering." Notice the sensible coping theme in these examples:

- "This light is tough, so I need to relax and feel more through my skis."
- "I almost fell, but my body tensing up is a cue to relax again now."
- "Well, everybody falls, and it isn't likely that I'll kill myself."
- "I can feel my muscles tensing. Normally I would interpret this as fear. It's not, though. It's just a reflexive response, and I can feel myself relaxing again."

Follow up   It is clear that our social system neglects to train us to praise ourselves. The caricature of the person shuffling his feet and saying, "Aw shucks, t'weren't nothin'," in response to genuine praise is a good example. Now is the time to change that. You have stopped the catastrophizing, evaluated and uprooted some unrealistic fears, and labeled them more appropriately. Now, compliment yourself! You are moving toward your goals.

- "Yeah! That helps me be more sensible."
- "I'm not so tense right now—feels good."
- "That old tension itself is beginning to cue me to figure out what I'm saying to myself. I'm doing fine!"
- "Hooray!"

Or say whatever works for you. Your progress is personally yours. Enjoy and compliment yourself as the mountain begins to ski you less.

S.E.L.F. Modification of Your Anger Monologues

Sometimes you may get impatient with yourself for an obvious error. At other times you may get angry at your psychology. It is interesting to observe this quirk in skiers: They may *know* they are psyching themselves out in certain situations and then worsen the problem by getting terribly impatient with themselves for doing so! If you are not aware of techniques to change your psychology, your anger persists. Finally it gets to the point where perhaps only half of the problem is caused by the original psych-out. The rest of the problem results from the futility you experience as you try harder to resolve it. The point we want to make is that the S.E.L.F. modification of anger yields a double benefit. Change your original impatient self-talk a bit and the rest will follow beautifully.

Stop your thoughts. As with your fear monologues, the conversation has to stop. Use the thought-stopping technique to decrease the perseverance of your frustration and anger.

Evaluate. Just what goal have you set for yourself that you are trying to reach with such painful futility? Especially where anger and impatience are concerned, evaluation and modification of your expectations are imperative. This goes back to the problem of setting yourself up to fail because you set your goals unrealistically high. You then fail and begin the "I told me so" recriminations.

I will not get tense. I will flow over every bump, setting edges, carving turns, rarely falling. My legs will be like shock absorbers; my skis will carve perfectly; I will be a model of smooth control of anything the mountain has to offer today. I am now about to begin a quietly competent assault on these bumps.

That was Pete in chapter 3, you may recall. Actually he could not ski with that kind of grace. He needed to change something!

Label. Here is how Pete got more sensible and relabeled:

I can relax. Let me relax for a moment or two. Okay, I will ski the next hundred yards and then stop from a position of balance. There's my line. I'll absorb the bumps on this section.

There was an immediate change in Pete's skiing. He did not yet ski as a model of smooth control, of course. He needed more technique pointers and more practice. But he skied at peace with himself, actively aware of his body and the terrain. He was meeting a new challenge and he was now ready, in the best sense of the word, for that further instruction.

Laura was experiencing the "expert blues." Normally a superb skier, she was for some reason having a series of bad days. She was complaining to her new skiing companion that she just did not normally ski this badly. But try as she might, she just could not show him her normal skiing. It became apparent that she was skiing for him, judging herself against the standards she perceived him to have, tensely determined to ski perfectly. A talk with him about her self-talk, plus some thought-stopping, evaluation of expectations, and more appropriate labeling freed her mind. Predictably, that one morning of active awareness and S.E.L.F. modification also freed up her skiing.

More than one skier has said to us, "Okay, if I change my standards for myself, where is the challenge?" We respond that it is there, and it is a greater challenge than before. You eliminate the challenge only if you never attempt to meet your standards. People with excessive standards stop trying *seriously* to reach them. The standards become like last New Year's resolutions, whose only function is to remind you of your failures to improve yourself. Your standards are your own, not those of your friends or of observers. The time to label more appropriately is when you are aware of self-critical responses to your skiing, aware of impatience, or aware of anger. At that point these feelings are blocking your skiing. Letting them go is certainly a challenge. And working your way back up to your goal without battering your head against it is even more of a challenge.

Follow up. It is reasonable to compliment yourself when you are doing better. But since many of us are not used to complimenting ourselves for "better," rather than "best," we forget to do it. Please do not forget. Complimenting yourself increases the probability you will successfully use that helpful tactic again. It is good for you. And it feels great, or at least, "better."

Additional Self-Talk

Here are some more thoughts about appropriate coping comments and strategies, together with a case illustration.

Fear and Courage as Labels

If you have taken a lesson recently, your instructor may have given the class some tips on how to deal with fear. He or she might have asked the class, "On a fear scale of 1 to 10, rate yourselves."

Instructors find this a useful tactic for helping students cope with fear because they believe that simply through the act of labeling fear, it diminishes. This may or may not be true. Nevertheless, the tactic can be used as part of a countering process that can also give you some insight into your performance under stress. This is how it is done. The next time you get into a tight spot and feel fearful, rate your *fear* on the 1–10 scale. Now ski. How well or poorly you do is unimportant. Just get to where you wanted to get, whether the end of the steep section, the end of the run, or the bottom of the mountain. When you have arrived, congratulate yourself! On a *courage* scale of 1–10, where are you? The higher you were on the fear scale, the higher you will be on the courage scale.

Coping Comments

These straightforward "counters" are further examples of those that have been used successfully by skiers with whom we have worked. Some counters dissolve self-criticism, some involve labels, and some are positive follow-ups.

- "Let's see—what is it I have to do to change my weight distribution in this wet snow?"
- "Everybody falls. I can progress faster if I relax and realize that."
- "My tension is my cue to stop and relax. I can feel myself relaxing more now."
- "She has been skiing for years. I'll get there, too. Now, relax and watch."
- "Just because they are psyched out is no reason for me to be psyched out. Don't prejudge the run."
- "Those turns felt beautifully balanced!"
- "I can learn this a step at a time if I quit picking myself apart. Let go of the tension."

Jeff's Case

Jeff was an advanced skier who could ski anywhere on the mountain, in any ski condition—*almost*. And that *almost* was most annoying to him. On powder days when the fresh stuff was getting skied out, his friends would head for the woods and dive into the untracked snow between the trees. But not Jeff. Just standing at the top of a tree run and looking down would make him very nervous. He told us about his problem in a session of a *Skiing Out of Your Mind* workshop.

"What do you mean by 'very nervous'?" we asked.

"You know. I can feel my heart thumping, I get butterflies in my stomach, I kind of breathe hard...I...I feel nervous."

"Yes. I know what you mean," one of us said. "I sometimes get similar feelings at the top of a super steep run. Even expert skiers have their limits, but we push them don't we? After all, that's where the big thrills are. And that's when the butterflies come."

"But I hate those feelings. I can't ski when I'm feeling like that."

"How do you know, if you avoid the conditions that bring them up?"

Jeff thought a moment. "I guess you're right. But I really hate having those feelings. What can I do to stop them?"

That was our cue. One of us said, "I'm not sure what can be done to stop them. On the other hand, perhaps you can look more closely at what the feelings mean."

"What do you mean?"

"Remember the fight or flight response... that part about emotional learning... that we talked about in the first section of the workshop? Those feelings you dislike are associated with that physiological response. It could be they are a signal from your body that it is primed to perform some strenuous physical activity, that you are ready for a challenge. Turning 'em in the trees is certainly a challenge." We were relabeling his fear response as the excitement that goes with a challenge.

"Hey," Jeff said, "That's a really interesting way to look at it. Let me think about it for a while."

Several weeks later we received a letter from Jeff. It read in part, "It took a while, but worked. When we got to the top of the tree run, I got those feelings again, but I remembered what I had rehearsed, and I said to myself, 'OK, Self, these feelings just mean that my body is primed for extra energy. I'm going to take that energy and use it to ski this run.' Well, it was great. I mean, I really had a tremendous amount of energy, and I skied that run as nicely as I had ever skied anything. And the feelings weren't so awful either. What a rush!''

For Jeff, more constructive thinking was a matter of interpretation. At some time in his past he had associated those feelings of physiological arousal with fear. When he stood at the top of a tree run (the unknown, for him) he imagined danger, which led to physiological arousal, which he felt and then labeled *fear*. But when he examined those feelings more objectively, he could understand that, for him, it was only *after* the onset of the feelings that the fear came into play. By relabeling them as a *rush*, and reminding himself that they were associated with a high energy state, he was able to go ahead and use that energy. Gradually the feelings were no longer experienced as unpleasant but merely as feelings. Moreover, he turned them into a reminder that he was physically ready to accept a challenge.

If you find yourself avoiding some snow condition or terrain even though you know realistically that you have the skills to handle it, analyze your reasons. Are they prompted by unpleasant feelings? Can these feelings be reinterpreted as your body's response for action, the adrenaline rush? If so, remind yourself that you have enough skills to handle this run and that you have a tremendous amount of energy available to you, and use it!

Exercises

1. As outlined earlier, gain some experience with thought-stopping.
2. Creating your personal counters (labels) is essential. Another way to think of this coping tactic is "putting a tail on the dog," where the "dog" can be any nonproductive or self-defeating thought and the tail can be an added realistic reappraisal. You can begin to do this off the

mountain by setting aside 5 or 10 minutes to sit back and relax. Recall and recapture the feelings during your recent bout with fear or frustration. Now, identify what you are/were saying to yourself and create several counters for each of those self-statements so you will be able to label differently. You might even wish to write them down if your self-talk is a major problem for you. Continue to do this as often as you can identify different disruptive self-statements and create a variety of counters.

3. As you are relaxing, recreate the above experiences. Feel them. Now apply in your imagination the counters you just made up in the S.E.L.F. sequence. Remember that S.E.L.F. should flow together. Practice this as often as reasonably possible. For example, you could do it several times a day instead of daydreaming.

4. Apply your S.E.L.F. sequence consistently and consciously the next few times you are skiing. If you are consistent for several days, you will find that the S.E.L.F sequence becomes much more automatic. You will be redefining your skiing and yourself.

CHAPTER 10

Concentration

One of the biggest problems in skiing, whether in competition or for recreation, is a lack of concentration. And one of the biggest obstacles to concentration is your mind. It can trip you up more easily than a patch of ice, a clump of wet snow, or an abrupt mogul. We all have some memories of a failure to concentrate. Here's one of ours:

Several seasons ago, I competed in an annual spring skiing race. Although the race was strictly for fun, it employed the same dual slalom elimination format that the professionals use on their circuit. After qualifying trials and elimination heats, I reached the finals. Concentrating on every turn, I was skiing well and felt confident. The first run of the finals was no different. I won by almost half a second. On the second run, I skied the upper part of the course well and pulled ahead by a couple of ski lengths. At that point I thought, "I'm ahead, I'll win." Instantly, I caught my ski in a rut and shot off course. My opponent sailed by to an easy victory. Seven and a half runs of perfect concentration, punctuated by one distracting thought, turning victory into defeat.

The next season, I entered the same race and again reached the finals. My technique was good. My only worry at that point was my concentration. Last year's mental lapse was a sharp memory. Before the start, I cleared my mind by focusing on the rhythm of my breathing. Then I played a surging tune in my mind to increase my sense of excitement and arousal. When I stood in the starting gate, I focused my awareness on the terrain in front of me and rehearsed the vision I would have as I skied each gate. My attention was on the course, not on the racer next to me. For each run I maintained that narrow focus on the course and did not widen it to include the other racer until I crossed the finish line. I won both runs comfortably. Victory was nothing compared to the experience of total concentration.

"Concentration" is one of the most overused and least understood terms in sports. Players, coaches, spectators, and sportscasters are fond of attributing victories and defeats alike to that elusive power. Yet, when told to concentrate, most performers become tense, distracted, or paralyzed. This is because concentrating is not something one can *do*. It is the *result* of doing something else, namely focusing attention.

Focused Attention

Downhill skiing is a relatively brief sport. That is, while you are actually skiing, very little time is passing. For most people, only 15 to 30 seconds elapse before they stop, pause, and decide where to ski next. Even racers normally spend no more than 2½ minutes skiing a downhill or giant slalom from start to finish. This means that while you are actually skiing you have very little time and therefore very little room for error. Your attention must be focused on what you are doing and nothing else.

Specifically, your attention must be on the interaction between your body and the terrain. The mechanism for this focus is your mind. Several things can affect the way your mind focuses on this interaction. First, your arousal level must be optimal. Recall the performance/arousal curve in chapter 1. If you are not very excited about your skiing, your mind will be attending to something more interesting (like wondering about the stock market) or more distracting (like your cramped feet). On the other hand, if you are too aroused, your mind will be attending to some aspect about the body/terrain interaction which also interferes with your performance (like how frightened you feel, how tense you are, or how worried you are about not doing well enough). The other chapters of this book address different channels of your mind to help you function at the optimal point on your performance/arousal curve. Mastering skills in relaxation, imagery, self-talk, and operant and vicarious learning will help you center yourself and your attention for peak performance.

In addition to centering yourself at the optimal point on your performance/arousal curve, there are other factors that help you focus on the interaction between your body and the terrain. One is knowing where to *begin* your focus. Another is knowing how to *maintain* it.

Beginning Focus

Most skiers begin their day without focus. They do not have any idea what they want to accomplish that day except perhaps to have fun, stay warm, or go back to the office with a tan. They take the lift to the top, maybe do some stretching exercises, and push off for their first run. They may end up making some good turns and thinking, "Boy, this is going to be a good day," only to catch an edge, thoroughly dust themselves with new-fallen snow, and decide that it is not going to be so good after all. Or they may start off with some bad turns, feel awkward, and conclude that this will be a good day to quit early. If skiers in either situation get some good skiing in, it will be purely by chance. And, as you know from the material on operant learning, that will happen just often enough to keep them coming back to begin the next day in a similarly unfocused and random way.

There is an alternative. First, have an idea of what you want to accomplish for your skiing, whether it is something specific like staying more on the fall line on steep runs or something more general like skiing more relaxed. Second, and most important, narrow your focus *before you start each section of each run.* That focus will usually begin inward and move outward.

Inner Focus   Start by attending to the sensations in your body. If you note any excess tension, do a tension check/release. Then attend to the sensations in your feet. Move your feet, boots, and skis and be aware of the kinesthetic response your muscles make to achieve and adjust to those movements. Now change your focus to your imagery. Visualize the way you want to be skiing, rehearse that image in your mind, and imagine your body moving accordingly.

If your goal for the day is to improve a particular physical skill, such as getting on and off your edges quickly, mentally rehearse your body doing that and start skiing. Do not attend to anything else while you are skiing. If your mind wanders, tune it back to the sensations of your feet moving quickly to set and release your edges. Do not worry about any other aspect of your skiing at that time. Remember that your goal is to work on edge control. In general, whenever you are working on a kinesthetic skill, you should begin with an inner focus and remain there. On the other hand, if you are working on your skiing in relation to some aspect of the terrain, you should begin with an inner focus and shift it outward before you start skiing each section.

Outer Focus After you have attended to your internal sensations and rehearsed yourself skiing the way you would like, switch your attention to the environment. Look at the terrain you will be skiing and pick the line you plan to follow. Unless you are racing, it does not matter if you do not follow the line exactly. Just be sure that you begin with an *intention* to ski a certain line.

As you get into the rhythm of your turns, keep your attention focused on where you are trying to go. Your skis will follow if you keep looking ahead. Too many skiers get thrown by ice, bumps, or soft snow because they are not looking ahead. They shift their attention to watching where their skis are rather than where their bodies are going, and thus they cannot anticipate changes in the terrain. Furthermore, there is a physical consequence of looking down rather than ahead. With your head down, it is difficult to keep your hips and chest forward enough to be centered over your skis, and the tails of your skis will slide out of the turns.

Maintaining Focus

Beginning each section with a specific kinesthetic and visual focus is an essential element of concentration. However, it is not the whole story. No matter how focused your attention is when you start, it will shift as new stimuli impinge on your awareness. If you are focused on your line of descent, for example, and you become aware that a lot of people are stopped on the trail, your focus may shift to wondering whether they are watching you. That momentary distraction is enough to cause you to miss a pole plant, lose your balance, and tumble spectacularly in full sight of all of them, thus answering your question in the affirmative. The problem here is not that you were momentarily distracted; we get distracted all the time. Rather, the problem is that you did not refocus on your line of descent before you missed your pole plant. The solution lies in your ability to rapidly switch stations in your mind.

Station Switching   Think of your mind as a radio receiver. Signals from many stations come in all at once, but your receiver is tuned in to only one of them so you are not aware of all the others. However, your tuner tends to drift from one station's signal to another's. Unlike a radio with automatic frequency control (AFC), your tuner does not automatically correct to hold you on that one station. You may start out with a clear, strong focus on the "music" of your rhythmic skiing, only to drift over to hard rock, cacophonous contemporary, soporific elevator music, or news and weather. If your mind is on one of those stations, your body will soon follow.

To develop your own AFC, practice the following exercise. Begin by focusing on the word "on" printed below.

on

You will notice that after a few seconds your attention will drift and you will be aware of other thoughts or images in your line of vision. Each time your attention shifts, switch back to the image of the word "on." Once you have developed the ability to refocus without straining your tuner, intentionally shift your focus to other words on the page and immediately switch back to "on" after each other word. You will notice that the more you consciously switch back, the stronger the image "on" becomes in your mind and the less distracting the other words are, even though you notice them.

Indoor Slalom Thus far you have been refocusing without moving. This would be fine if your sport were archery, riflery, or darts. However, since skiing requires concentration while moving, you need some practice at that as well. Stand up. Hold your hands in front of you as though you were carrying ski poles. Begin by narrowing your visual focus to the doorway of the room you are in. (Skiing is the process of moving your body through openings, e.g., between bumps, rocks, people, slalom poles. We want you to focus on the space *between* things. The things will take care of themselves if you attend to the spaces.)

In a moment, we want you to start moving forward, slowly at first, aiming your body at the open spaces in the building. Any time you notice an object in your field of vision, switch your attention to the space around it. You will be aware of tables, chairs, lamps, and doorjambs, but you should focus on moving between them. You are not trying to get anywhere in particular; just keep moving forward, changing directions as necessary to move through the open spaces. As you do this, you will become less aware of the objects per se and more aware of the spaces. Pick up speed until you are moving at a fast walk or a jog. Keep your vision focused forward, look-ing past where you are seeking open spaces. Ready? Go. If you find that you are drifting to some focus other than open spaces, stop. Do a tension check/release, retune your atten-tion to the next open space, and begin again.

This exercise can be even more effective outdoors if there is a grove of trees with just enough space for you to move between them. Racers call this dry-land slalom. Although they do it primarily for quickness training, it works because it requires concentration while moving. The next time you are on skis, set an imaginary slalom course on the terrain in front of you, for example between gentle bumps. Do not worry about your ski technique; this is an exercise in concentration. Focus your visual attention on the open spaces between bumps. Keep looking ahead while you are skiing. If you get distracted, stop, refocus, and begin again.

Putting Your Mind Where Your Body Is Occasionally you will become so distracted in your skiing that refocusing does not work, no matter how much you try. Your body is moving down the slope but your mind is elsewhere. You may be attending to something unrelated to your skiing, such as where you will have dinner tonight, or you may be attending to something related but dysfunctional (to your skiing), such as the attractive skier in front of you in the one-piece suit. Neither is an inappropriate focus for your attention; they just do not do much to improve your body's interaction with the terrain.

When you are so distracted that you cannot refocus your mind where your body is, do the reverse. Stop your body and let it assist your mind. Stop skiing and focus on the distracting thought or image. Consider in detail all your choices for dinner and stay focused on that until it no longer holds your attention. Or focus all your attention on that attractive skier. Watch intently until that person is out of sight. If you cannot bear to lose sight of the person, go after him or her. At least, you will have a goal now that holds your attention!

Concentration and Racing

If you are a racer, you know how important concentration is. This chapter began with just one small sample of the difference it makes between success and failure. Concentration applies equally well to racing as to recreational skiing. The important difference is that racers have even less room for error than do recreational skiers. Of course you know this and therefore try to focus your attention acutely during a race. But what about your practice? We know that the primary means of learning something is through rehearsal. The more you repeat something, the more it is wired into your muscles and nerves. If you practice racing without concentration, your muscles and nerves will learn movement without focus. Therefore it is crucial that you focus your attention *especially* during practice. Not only should you be doing the exercises in this chapter off the snow, but you should also be applying them every time you ski.

If your coach does not already do so, ask him or her to include focusing exercises as part of every workout. Be sure to begin every practice run with an inner and outer focus and complete every course with your focus narrowed to your line of descent. This is important even if you ski off the course or fall. If that happens, quickly refocus your attention on the course and finish. While you may be out of a race if you fall, you are never out of a practice. Your muscles and nerves are still learning something.

Many years ago, the Dartmouth ski team was doing no better than second place in the Eastern college circuit. The problem was the slalom. Despite having one of the best Alpine teams around, our top two or three racers would invariably lose concentration, blow out of the course, and put the team in a hole. Practices were little different. Although our skiers would turn in some blistering runs, we would just as often miss gates or fall and fail to finish the course. The team captain, recognizing that this transferred over to race days, exhorted us to finish no matter how badly we missed gates or fell. This idea did not set well with a team that was more interested in perfecting speed than in being consistent.

"Lighten up," we urged. "It's only practice."

"Precisely," he replied. "And we need to practice finishing."

Grumbling, we did as he asked, day after frustrating day. We were about ready to give up the whole idea until we got to the Eastern Championships, the meet that qualified teams for the NCAA Championships. The slalom course was one of the tightest of the season. No one said anything. We all knew what we had to do. After the first run, many racers had failed to finish, yet only one of ours had fallen. And the remainder of our racers were confident; we had wired-in our concentration in practice, so now we could focus on our turns, not our survival. We all finished the second run, and with superb times. We won the Eastern and were off to the NCAAs, thanks in no small part to a persistent team captain.

Exercises

1. Do an active awareness analysis of your lapses in concentration to pinpoint where and when (outer contexts) they occur. Do the same for your thoughts and feelings (inner contexts).
2. Use mental rehearsal to imagine yourself skiing *through* the points at which you break concentration.

3.   Each time you are on snow, seek out those outer contexts and recreate the inner contexts that accompany losses of concentration. Start with a mental focus on those contexts and then narrow your attention down to the line you plan to ski. Focus on the spaces (between people, bumps, gates). Then begin skiing slowly. While maintaining your focus on those spaces, pick up speed. If you lose concentration, slow down until you can refocus and pick up speed again.

CHAPTER 11

Metaphors: Connections Between Your Mind and Your Body

For some of you, it is sufficient to use your visual and kinesthetic channels to enhance your performance. You observe a good model, imagine yourself in that person's body, rehearse the sensations and, *voila*, your skiing is changed! But what if you are primarily a thinker rather than a feeler? What if you tend to use your "left-brain" (metaphorically speaking) more than your "right"? Your primary channel is cognitive. When you try to visualize or feel, little happens and you find yourself *thinking*, "What do I do now?" You need a bridge between the different channels of your consciousness, something to translate your thoughts into a language your body can sense. For centuries, poets have used metaphors to elicit emotional responses through literal words. "Champagne powder." "Carved turns." "Light as air." "Legs of steel." These are all figures of speech that give words a feeling beyond the literal meaning of the words themselves. An image is created, not through a visual or kinesthetic channel but through a cognitive one.

We use metaphors in skiing because they are an efficient way of getting from the mental experience of the mind to the physical experience of the body and back again. Through metaphors, you can create a new skiing experience. Once you have created that experience, you have material for new mental rehearsal, which reinforces the experience and wires it into your consciousness. Thus, metaphors are an aspect of mental imagery; they allow you to translate thought into action. The result is an integration between your mind and your body.

Beginning Metaphors

A Body Made for Skiing

For beginning skiers, putting on skis is like starting life all over again. Walking is out, skiing is in. Being hobbled by heavy boots fastened to cumbersome planks can be a humiliating experience for a body used to moving by putting one foot in front of the other. Instead of having feet that represent approximately 12 to 15% of our height, the body that we take skiing has feet as long as we are, giving us the shape of an inverted T. We need some metaphors to adjust our minds to this new body. One of the most useful is to experience your feet operating the way they need to with skis on. The following exercise is designed for that purpose.

Sit straight in a chair with your feet flat on the floor and parallel to each other. They don't need to be touching, but they shouldn't be more than 9 inches apart. Imagine your feet are a car and that on the floor in front of you is an S-shaped highway. Your toes are the front wheels of your car. Your objective is to steer your toes along the curves of the highway as it passes beneath your feet. Remember that your feet must work in unison. At first, look at your feet as you do this. Then close your eyes and feel yourself steer your feet in unison. Do this for 2 or 3 minutes. Add some hills and valleys in the road. Follow these with your feet, picking them up off the floor as necessary.

Imagine that your feet have grown and your toes are actually 6 inches beyond the ends of your feet. Continue to steer them over the curving, hilly highway for another minute or two. Really feel your toes out there. Now imagine that your toes are 12 inches out in front of the ends of your feet. Keep steering them. When you are comfortable with your toes way out there, extend them another 24 inches. Really sense what it is like to have control over your toes 3 feet out from your body! Continue to steer them up, over, and around that curving, hilly road for another minute or two.

If you ask people what makes a ski turn, they are apt to say, "The side camber," "No, the edges," "No, the flex of the ski." These answers are not really correct. Steering your feet and twisting your legs makes your skis turn. The preceding exercise gets you to experience steering your feet instead of trying to turn your skis.

It also gets you to experience your feet being as long as your skis, making your skis an extension of your body. You should practice this metaphor daily for about 5 minutes until you can really experience what it is like to have your toes in the tips of your skis. When you go skiing, carry that experience with you. Practice it on the chairlift by closing your eyes and steering your "toes" (ski tips) over the imaginary curving highway passing below you. When you are actually skiing, continue this metaphor on a smoothly packed slope that is not too steep. As you experience it, you will be concentrating on your skiing. In fact, when you are really experiencing, the concentration is automatic.

Reframing a Friendly Environment

Unless you ski every day, the habits of skiing probably will not become natural. This means that whenever you go skiing you are entering a foreign environment, one that requires you to act in alien ways. Much of the alienation in skiing is due to the way you construe this ski environment. Except for those experts who view all conditions as a beckoning challenge, most skiers encounter conditions that they dread more than welcome. For many skiers, large moguls and deep powder are two of the most dangerous conditions in skiing. Yet they can be friendly if viewed through a new framework. For this, you need to be open-minded about them. *Reframing* your view through metaphors can facilitate this new attitude.

Bumps When confronted with a slope of big moguls, what do you usually see? One friend of ours visualizes a "field of tank traps." Another sees "huge teeth, waiting to grind me up." Neither of these images is very conducive to a friendly relationship with the mountain. On the other hand, you can also view the bumps as a giant staircase built for your graceful descent. Instead of being a tank trap, the uphill side of each mogul provides a platform for your turn, making the slope less steep. Imagining the bumps in this way allows you to use them to your advantage rather than be intimidated by them (which produces anxiety, tension, and avoidance).

If you are fighting the bumps, the action of skiing moguls can also be different. Some skiers feel that when they go over bumps, the mountain is like a bronco trying to buck them off their skis. A more friendly metaphor is to think of the action of the bumps as caressing your skis and massaging your legs. Because they are friendly touches, you want to caress them back by moving your skis lightly over their crests, almost like waves. If viewed this way, skiing bumps becomes an action of retracting your legs to allow the bump to pass beneath you.

Powder Skiing in powder, whether 6 inches deep or 60, is like entering another universe. It can produce either an incredible "high" or a miserable depression. You can feel as though you are floating or drowning.

We use the water image here intentionally. The best metaphor that we have for skiing powder is being in water. Most people have difficulty with powder because they fight it. They feel unnatural in the snow because they are used to skiing *on* it. Trying to ski on top of powder snow is like trying to swim on top of the water. If you fight it, you will sink. But if you let yourself be in it, you will find that it supports you. Once you stop fighting powder snow, you will notice that it requires less effort than skiing on hard-pack, especially if it is steep.

Powder can be a floating experience. Although the technique is obviously different, the sensation is like bodysurfing. You need to let yourself be in the snow and let it support and carry you just as you are supported and carried by the water. If you don't struggle against it, the snow will begin to buoy your skis as you accelerate, just as water buoys your body.

The next time you venture off into the deep, approach it with the same interest and enthusiasm with which you approach swimming. This is not to say there is nothing more to powder skiing than being in water. Powder-skiing technique is best learned from an instructor. The metaphor is designed for your mind, to let your body get in there and learn instead of fighting the snow.

Rhythm as a Bridge

Have your ever watched a freestyle ski competition? For the ballet event the competitors select a piece of music to accompany their performance, just as in figure skating or gymnastic floor exercises. Music and rhythm are integral aspects of human movement. They are also part of the peak experiences in skiing. Music psychs up your emotions and rhythm coordinates your movements.

Many skiers have discovered this for themselves. They hum their favorite melody as they glide along a gentle ski run. But when they get to a difficult section of the trail, the music stops and the fear-talk often takes over. In composing the musical "The King and I," Rodgers and Hammerstein showed that they understood a lot more about human consciousness than most skiers when they wrote "Whistle a Happy Tune." The lyric describes the use of a rhythmic melody for coping with a fear-arousing situation. Music seems to block out thoughts about fear. This may be because of the complementary nature of the right and left sides of the brain. Dr. Robert Ornstein and others believe that we alternate between functions of the right and left brain instead of using them simultaneously. Thus, it may be that when you are experiencing right-brain phenomena (like rhythm and music), there is less likelihood that left-brain phenomena (like angry or fearful self-talk) will interfere with your skiing. In other words, concentration on a right-brain activity like the feeling of skiing appears to be more compatible with another right-brain activity (music) than with a left-brain activity (linear thinking). You should be aware that these explanations are hypotheses, not scientific facts. However, the phenomenon is real. Rhythm improves performance.

And the more difficult the terrain, the more you need rhythm to perform at your peak.

The Beat of Different Drummers

Anne was an advanced intermediate skier who typically made graceful linked turns down the slope—until she got to a steep pitch. There she would stop, traverse, sideslip, make one turn, traverse some more, and become tense despite her ability to ski directly down any pitch the mountain had to offer. The problem was not in her technique; it was in her rhythm, or lack of it. Her instructor told her she was not turning frequently enough. He suggested that he follow her and instruct her to turn whenever he thought she should. As soon as she started down the next steep pitch he said, "Turn." Immediately after she completed her first turn, he said again, "Turn," and repeated "Turn, turn, turn" behind her down the slope. When she reached the bottom, she was euphoric. For the first time, she had skied directly down the fall line of a steep slope and had done it masterfully. On the next run, he suggested that she instruct herself by saying, "Turn, turn, turn, turn," aloud at frequent regular intervals. She did so with equally pleasant results. On the following run, she repeated the word to herself and skied the fall line with new confidence.

The instruction to turn was not the significant factor here. Anne already knew how and when to turn. The problem was that her anxiety about steep slopes had blocked her rhythm. By listening and then saying the regular sound of the word "turn," she was establishing a rhythm for both her mind and her body. The rhythm for her body enabled her to make linked fall-line turns. The rhythm for her mind maintained her concentration and prevented her left brain from interfering with experience-destroying thoughts.

We want to emphasize the importance of this last point. It is difficult, if not impossible, to turn off the thinking part of your brain. Your brain is working full-time unless you are unconscious. Rather than disconnect your brain from your experience, we suggest that you integrate the two by consciously providing rhythmic and metaphoric experiences for your mind.

Dancing Together

One other way of establishing rhythm is to pick up the beat of another skier, especially in difficult terrain. It has been our experience that the follow-me approach models a rhythm as much as it does a particular ski technique. There is only one caveat in this process: Contrary to what many skiers would have you believe, there are many different rhythms to skiing. If you happen to follow a model whose rhythm is different from yours, you destroy your own timing and flow. Instead of improving, you will get worse. Those of you who have experienced the frustration of skiing behind a model who is outside your rhythm know what we mean. For those of you who have not, it is like trying to waltz with someone who is doing the fox-trot. Occasionally the consequences are worse than just stepping on someone else's toes. If you follow directly behind someone, his or her rhythm becomes an unavoidable part of the gestalt. You are stuck with it for those turns whether it fits or not.

The only way to discover whether you and someone else have the same tempo is to "dance" together. Try to follow that person's example. You will know if it does not fit because you will feel more awkward with each run. If that happens, do not force it. You can still benefit from the other person's modeling. Stand still and observe, experience, and imitate. You will also know if the follow-me approach does fit. You will find yourself flowing with the other person. Without your thinking, your movements will parallel the model's. You will feel it.

Whatever your own source of rhythm, we encourage you to include it in your skiing. Some people have found that the counterpoint of baroque music makes a nice accompaniment to their bump skiing. We have a friend who takes Strauss waltzes with her whenever she skis powder. Another friend plays rock music in his head for blasting through the crud. Everyone skis to the beat of a different drummer. It does not matter whether you play an elaborate symphony in your mind or merely repeat a single sound; the important point is that you facilitate your performance with rhythm. When you are doing this, you need not turn to the exact beat of the music. When and where you turn depends on the terrain as much as it does on your intention and your music. In fact, in some situations such as racing, you would not want to play music while actually skiing. Music is a vehicle for getting in tune with the mountain. It gears your mind for a rhythmic experience.

A Few Metaphors for Getting Out of a Rut

We have found that when skiers are stuck in a rut in their progress they are usually stuck in a rut in their minds. By reframing their view of themselves they are able to experience themselves and their skiing in a new way. This opens them to new learning. For any rut (problem) in skiing there is probably an infinite number of ways (metaphors) to reframe it and reexperience it. We offer you a few that have been effective with our students for solving specific problems.

Problem Ruts and Metaphoric Solutions

Problem: Too anxious or too listless (too much or too little arousal on the performance/arousal curve).

Ski Like a Happy Clown   Imagine you are a clown on skis and your job is to entertain children. Let yourself feel happy. Put on a smiley face. Laugh out loud at nothing in particular. Start acting silly. Remember, you have to make those kids laugh. When you are really feeling silly, ski it. Ski in a backward wedge, on one ski, wave your arms, jump, fall. Be as outrageous as you can. Don't forget to laugh!

Ski Like a Sad Clown   Now that you have them rolling in the aisles with your silliness, imagine that you are a sad sack. Really feel miserable. Imagine that everybody gets to you. Remember the old George Kelly clown role? Ski him. Feel down and out. Moan and wail. Try to get others to feel sorry for you.

Karate Skiing   Imagine that you have a black belt in karate. If you've ever seen a karate tournament, you know how the contestants take a few moments before the contest to quiet their minds, to center themselves. Even if you don't know what that means, pretend you do. See yourself as quick and powerful, with great energy in your legs. Look for any small bump, depression, or pile of snow, ski to the top of it, and with a loud karate yell, jump it. Each yell should be like an explosion, coming from your gut. EEYAH! Do it. Get springs in your legs. If this seems too difficult for you at first, just jump in place. When you feel comfortable with that, progress to jumping when you're sliding, then to small bumps. Don't forget to give your karate yell. EEYAH!

Aggressive Skiing Now that you have become a black belt at karate skiing, you can begin to work on relabeling your fear. Start by working yourself up to an aggressive state. Recall some instance or situation that makes you angry. It may be getting stuck in traffic; it may be an overbearing boss or an incompetent employee. Focus on your anger. Really work it up. Growl—GRR! Not like a pussy cat, like a tiger! Hear yourself roar. Let it out. Now ski. Chase those bumps—GRR! Start each turn with a growl—GRROWR! Finish each turn with a roar.

When you can really feel and act these roles, take a break and review how you skied differently with the different emotions. Continue skiing on comfortable terrain. Get a good run going, this time as yourself, and without stopping, switch to happy skiing, then to sad skiing, then to karate skiing, then to aggressive skiing. Notice how your energy level changes as you switch your emotions. Notice how it affects your skiing. Remember, these are exercises in feelings, so style and technique do not count.

So far, you have been practicing skiing to these emotions on easy slopes. If you are ready, start working your way to more difficult runs. Be careful here. Do not exceed your technical skill level but do challenge yourself emotionally. See if you can overcome fear by switching to a more aggressive state. When you get to the top of a steep pitch, don't stop, or you will only be making it harder for yourself. Continue your growling or karate yells as you ski over it. And by all means, enjoy yourself.

Here are more metaphors for changing your arousal level. Try them. See if they get you out of the rut. If not, make up your own.

- Ski like a mouse.
- Ski like a bear.
- Ski like your boss.
- Ski like your secretary.
- Ski like your spouse.

Problem: No rhythm.

Float Like a Butterfly, Sting Like a Bee   This may be one of the most famous metaphors of this generation. Muhammed Ali's description of his style is highly appropriate for skiing. Float through the middle of the turn, sting the snow to finish.

Dancing   Imagine that you are on a dance floor and the band is playing your favorite number. Hear the music in your mind. Pick up the rhythm and dance your way down the slope.

Problem: Knees and ankles stiff or frozen in the bumps.

Lights on Your Knees   Start on a bump run that is easy for you. Since you will be doing a series of traverses, stand on one side of the hill. Imagine that you have powerful spotlights on your knees. Turn them on and illuminate the slope in front of you. Adjust where they shine by flexing, extending, and twisting your legs. Push off. Go slowly enough to allow time for you to aim your knee lights in the direction you wish to go. See them point at the trough between the bumps on your right, then to your left, and so on, shining them on the line you wish to be following just ahead.

Problem: Difficulty with short-radius turns down the fall line.

Lights on Your Shoulders   Starting on a run that does not give you trouble with fall-line skiing, imagine that you have search-lights on your shoulders. Turn them on. Shine them into the woods on your right. Point them downhill, then into the woods on your left. Have a friend ski downhill from you and stop about 15 yards away. Tell your friend to point to where you should shine your lights. Start skiing. Shine your lights where your friend directs. Imagine that your shoulder lights are illuminating the areas on which they are shining. If they're in the woods, yell out, "Woods." If downhill, yell out "Down," and so forth.

When you are on your own, pay attention to where your shoulder lights are shining. Start with wide-radius turns, with your shoulder lights shining in the general direction of your skis. Gradually change to short radius, focusing your shoulder lights more and more downhill. Work on remembering to check where your lights are shining as you ski. Consciously try to shine them downhill more and more.

Problem: Turns are too abrupt and ragged.

Alphabet Turns For many intermediate skiers, allowing the skis to work through a turn is difficult. The feeling of acceleration as the skis get into the fall line is a little frightening. They feel as though they are losing control. This often results in hurrying the skis through the middle of the turn, leaving a track that looks like a Z. This habit develops on steeper slopes and often remains, even after speed and feelings of loss of control are no longer a problem. One way to get out of this rut is to play with alphabet turns. As you ski, make your tracks into letters: C, S, Z, J, L.

Falling Leaf After you have initiated a turn, imagine that you are a falling leaf, caught in a gentle autumn breeze. Let the breeze carry you through the middle of the turn without any further turning effort on your part.

Gravity Turns From a traverse on moderate terrain, flatten your skis on the snow. Don't apply any turning forces. Let gravity gradually pull your skis into the fall line, beginning with your tips. As you cross the fall line, gently finish the turn.

Problem: Over-rotation of upper body, too little upper/lower body separation.

Martini Tray This is a classic. Imagine that you are carrying a tray of martinis down the slope. Hold the tray with both hands in front of you, and more or less downhill. Imagine the tray with its drinks as vividly as possible. As you ski, hear the glasses rattle; see the liquid shake. Be careful, don't spill any!

Hockey Stops Another classic. Imagine you are a hockey player, rapidly approaching the boards. Hold your poles together in one hand, as though they were the stick. In stopping, twist your skis and lower body in one direction, your upper body and the "stick" in the other. See how much "ice" you can spray as you are doing this.

Problem: Too little edge control.

Edging by the Numbers This was introduced in the "inner game" era. Imagine a rating scale for the angle of your ski to the snow. Keep your range low. If a flat ski is 0, make a completely edged ski 3 or 4. Experiment with shifting from one number to the other and notice the effect on skis and turns.

Herringbone This is the classic uphill walk. Everyone should do this once in a while.

Pour Water From Boot to Boot We love this one, especially on a cold day. Imagine filling your boots with hot water. As you turn, imagine tipping the boot of the outside ski into the boot of the inside ski and transferring water into it. Since the water is hot, imagine you can feel the warmth rise in the filled boot ("Ahhh") and get lower in the emptying boot ("Brr").

Show Ski Bottoms Imagine that you have a message written on the bottom of your skis. You must give this message to a courier below you on the hill. While turning, do whatever it takes to get your skis on edge enough so that the courier can see the bottoms of your skis.

Problem: Too little control of ski pressure, knees too flexed, too little leg extension.

Bobbing This one works well for skin divers. As you stand on the hill, imagine that you are standing neck deep in water (warm, of course). Duck your head under and exhale as you do. Now rise, bring your head above the surface, and inhale. Practice this bobbing/breathing maneuver before you ski. Then ski, rising/inhaling as you begin each turn, gradually sinking/exhaling as you cross the fall line and finish. In super-deep powder this is an effective way to avoid inhaling a lungful of snow.

Bicycling   Everyone knows how to ride a bike. Imagine that your skis are bike pedals, and as you push on the pedal, *that* leg gets longer while the other gets shorter.

Rocket Launchers   Imagine that you are a rocket and that you are launching straight *up* by pushing both legs straight *down*.

Your Own Metaphors

A word of caution. Some of our metaphors may not work for you, and you will be tempted to say, "This is crazy! Metaphors don't help skiing." We want you to know that these metaphors work for us and other skiers we know. If they do not work for you, the problem is not with the idea of metaphors, nor is it with you. Rather, it is with these metaphors. In that case, try to discover your own. When you have found a metaphor that works, your mind will experience your body's sensations. Recall a perfect day of skiing. As you reexperience that day (or any other time you had a good turn or a good run, or handled a difficult condition for the first time), notice what your mind is sensing. If you are really into the experience, you may notice that images appear. You may feel yourself drifting under water or soaring above the earth. Or you may be experiencing something unrelated to skiing or physical activity at all. Whatever images you experience are your metaphors. They are the ways your mind perceives the sensations of your body. By recalling and reexperiencing those images when you are not skiing, you are preparing your mind and body for when you are skiing.

CHAPTER 12

Falling Out
of Your Mind

F alling. All of the awkwardness in skiing, all of the bad survival habits, and all of the tension, both reflexive and voluntary, are intended to do one thing: to keep you from falling. And why not? There are many reasons to try to avoid falling. Here are some of them:

- You might get hurt.
- You might get wet or cold.
- You might hurt someone else.
- Other people might think you are not very good.
- You might think you are not very good.
- You might feel embarrassed.
- Your inner ear and autonomic nervous system are trying to keep you upright.
- You might lose time.
- You might lose the race.
- Your friends might get tired of waiting for you.

All of these are good reasons for not falling. They are also good reasons for not going skiing. The best way to be certain you will not fall is to stay home. If you go skiing, you are going to fall. The two are inseparable. Like it or not, the gravity that causes you to fall also pulls you down the mountain as you ski.

Actually, skiing begins with a fall. In order to start your skis down the slope you must cause your upper body and hips to fall forward. However, you avoid landing on your body by bringing your skis along with you. A fall occurs when your feet and skis move at a different rate or in a different direction from the rest of your body. So the best way to keep yourself from falling is to keep your feet and skis under you. Another expression for having your feet under you is "having balance."

Essentially, skiing is *balanced* falling. This becomes obvious if you watch downhill skiers such as Austrian champion Franz Klammer. His gold medal run in the 1976 Olympic downhill was a beautiful example of staying within the boundaries of balance while "falling" down the course at an incredible rate of speed. Although he appeared to be out of control to many observers, he was in almost complete balance as he used gravity to produce the ultimate in speed.

It's our guess that you do not consider balanced falling to be a problem. In fact, you'd probably like a little more balance in your falling. We are making this point to stress the importance of falling in skiing. Most skiers think that skiing is the opposite of falling, that to do the former you should avoid the latter. When you try not to fall, what happens? You fall, of course.

There are basically four causes of falling. The first two concern physics. One of them is gravity, and you can't change that. The second is faulty balance. (Though this problem is outside the scope of our book, there are many ways to improve your balance. One of the best is to practice gymnastics.)

The other two major causes of falling are psychological. One is too much tension. If you are reading this book from front to back, you already know how and why tension affects your skiing and what to do about it. The fourth cause of falling is too much relaxation. This is characteristic of skiers who send their brains out for a beer, leaving themselves mindless for the rest of the day. Although these skiers rarely get hurt, they fall a lot, usually more than the tense ones. Unfortunately, they do not learn much from their falls. (How can they? Their learning apparatus is down in the bar.) But they are having so much fun that they probably do not mind anyway. If you are this type of skier, we are happy to leave you to your falls.

The last thing we want to do is interfere with someone else's fun.

Tension is a problem, however. Tense falls are *psychologically* unpleasant because if you are tense, you are trying *not* to fall and have failed by falling. Tense falls are *physically* more dangerous as well because you are more apt to injure yourself than if you are relaxed. And the tension triggered at a fall, although it is reflexive and natural, prevents you from learning anything from the fall. If you can minimize some of the tension, each fall will become a valuable step toward improvement.

Tension and Falling

Most beginners and intermediate skiers are tense when they fall, and with good reasons. Since we think falling can be beneficial, let's look at these good reasons as well as some ideas for changing the labels in your S.E.L.F. modification.

1. Fear of getting hurt. This is always a possibility in skiing. That is part of what makes it a risk sport. The best protections against this are, first, good safety bindings, adjusted by a knowledgeable binding mechanic in a ski shop or ski department, and second, the courage to say no when you cannot do something. The odds of getting hurt under those two conditions are negligible. Knowing this can take the fear out of your falls and let you learn something from them.
2. Fear of getting cold and wet. It is reasonable to worry about this only if you are not wearing adequate clothing. Money invested in good ski clothing is money well spent.
3. Fear that you might hurt someone else. You can avoid this more easily by skiing under control than by not falling. This means not going closer to another skier than 15 feet and stopping below skiers standing in the trail.
4. Fear that other people may think you are not very good. Only someone who has never skied before will think that a fall represents bad skiing. All skiers fall. If anyone is going to judge you by your skiing, he or she will base that

judgment on the way you ski when you are standing up, not on the way you look falling down.

5. Fear that you might think you are not very good. The answer for this is the same as for number 4.

6. You might feel embarrassed. Number 4 again. If you really feel that falling is something to be embarrassed about, you have not realized that all skiers fall. Furthermore, as Gestalt therapist Fritz Perls said, "Being embarrassed is getting caught at something you like."

7. Fear that your autonomic nervous system does not like being upside down. So what? You overcame your resistance to falling down and learned to walk, didn't you? Besides, the snow is a lot nicer to fall on than the kitchen floor.

8. Fear that you might lose time. Where's the fire? Unless you're in a race, you are not going to miss anything by falling down a few times.

9. Fear that you might lose the race. If you are in a race, your objective is to go as fast as you can without falling. That means that you are trying to be right on the edge of falling, and sometimes you miss. But that is part of the sport of ski racing. You would not be there if you were not willing to take the risk of falling. Furthermore, as we discuss below, falling in ski race *training* can be useful and even necessary in some cases.

10. Fear that your friends might tire of waiting for you. Don't laugh at this one. We know quite a few skiers who are very sensitive about keeping their friends waiting. If you are one of them, you might want to check it out by asking them. If it really bothers you, you have two choices: You can ski by yourself or with someone else who is slower paced, or you can tell your friends to go on ahead and you will either catch up or meet them in the lift line.

Fun and Falling

Remember how much fun it was as a child to throw yourself into a snowbank or tumble down a hill of sand or jump into a pile of leaves? There is real joy in throwing yourself off balance intentionally and knowing that you're going to land safely. Consider diving into a swimming pool. You actually fall in under control because your upper body moves ahead of your feet. Or consider carnival rides; the more disorienting the "fall," the more popular the ride. Falling is fun so long as you are not afraid of the catastrophes we addressed in the previous section—or of any others that you create in your mind.

To be able to enjoy falling in skiing, you must work up to it. The basic principle underlying working up to falling is the same as that underlying working up to anything you fear: Do it one step at a time (see chapter 8). The following is an exercise to help you decrease your tension and increase your comfort with falling.

First of all, you must know where to fall. There are two locations you should take into account: the place on the mountain, and the place on your body. For your first intentional fall, pick a place on the slope where there are no rocks, stumps, trees, or ice, and preferably one with a slight grade. Pick a place on your body where you have some padding. *With skis off*, sit down in the snow. Before you get too comfortable, get up and do it again. Get up and do it a third time. You have just taken three falls. Nothing to write home about, but not bad for starters. Now roll a little when you fall, adding some motion. Put your skis on and repeat the falls.

Now for a moving fall, begin with skis off. Make sure you do this on a slope with a moderate grade and soft-packed snow. Start by running and rolling a few times. Then put your skis on. With your skis on, your fall should be just like a baseball player's feet-first slide into second base. While moving, hold your poles up out of the way and sit down on your hips and back. Keep your feet up so your skis don't catch in the snow as you slide. Repeat this several times until you can do it without tension. You are doing it without tension when you are truly loose enough to sit down like a puppet whose strings have been cut. This is falling like the Scarecrow in chapter 5. Practice falling until you get to that point.

Now *sense* how you are feeling. Intense? Silly? Awkward? Joyful? *Are you having any fun?* If not, you are still too attached to being upright and you are taking yourself too seriously. Remember how much fun you had playing in the snow as a kid? Adopt that metaphor and repeat the exercises from a 6-year-old's point of view. Let yourself get to know the snow. Roll in it, taste it, smell it, feel it. It will not bite, and it will not let you down when you fall.

If snow is not available and you want to practice falling anyway, you can repeat these exercises on a bed, a pile of pillows, or soft grass. If you are outside, wearing your boots and poles can make the experience even more real. It will also make it easier for you to laugh at yourself.

Why are we encouraging you to enjoy falling? Obviously, we do not recommend it as the preferred way to stop. And we are not suggesting that you try to fall. We just want you to be relaxed about falling. Being able to enjoy falling is important for several reasons. First of all, if you can realize that falling is fun and is a natural part of skiing, you will not be so likely to punish yourself when you do fall. Second, by giving yourself permission to fall and enjoy it, you free yourself from trying not to fall so much. Finally, of course, the tension is not blocking you from learning anymore.

Racing and Falling

Falling is more of a problem in ski racing than in almost any other sport. If you fall in a race, you are out. There is no tenth inning, no second half, no time left to recover and make up the difference. A ski race is like a sprint in track. The difference between winning and losing is measured in hundredths of a second. But unlike a sprint, falling is common, even likely, in skiing. Based on this analysis you might think that the primary objective in ski racing is to avoid falling. Wrong. Making that the primary objective would be a mistake for two reasons: First, as we have explained before, if your primary goal is to prevent a fall, you will reflexively be stiff and tense and will not ski well or fast. Second, in order not to fall, even if you are not tense, you must ski more slowly than your peak performance level. And since races are won and lost by fractions of seconds, you will be out of the running if you are skiing slowly enough to guarantee that you will not fall. On the other hand, the objective is not to have so much fun with falling that you fall a lot. You might be enjoying yourself, but your coach, teammates, and sponsors would be displeased.

The answer to this problem lies in your practice, not in your racing. To fall or not to fall is irrelevant on race day. When you are in the race, even when you are in the starting gate, your attention should be on your turns and your speed. On the other hand, during practice your attention should be on your falls. Because peak racing performance means that you must be carrying your speed right up to the limit of the forces of physics, you need to find that limit. To know where that limit is, you must exceed it some of the time. If you do not fall very often in practice, you are not close enough to that limit. Conversely, if you are falling frequently in practice, you are too far over the limit. This limit is equivalent to the peak in your performance/arousal curve; for purposes of this discussion, speed replaces arousal.

Several years ago, we consulted with a ski coach who was concerned that, as he put it, "I have two kinds of slalom racers on this team. Those who place well when they stand up but who fall a lot in races, and those who hardly ever fall but also never place well." We helped him to recognize that his racers were distributed on either side of the performance/speed curve, and we devised a training program that set "falling" goals for those on each side. For the racers who were not skiing fast enough to reach their speed limits, we suggested a falling goal of 50% falls in practice. This meant that they had to push for more speed until they were exceeding their limits half of the time. This allowed them to develop the kinesthetic sense of how close they were to the edge of falling. For the racers who were exceeding their limits, we asked them to back off their speed and make rounder turns so that they were able to finish at least 90% of their practice runs without a fall.

If you are a racer, incorporate a falling plan into your training. Ask yourself how often you fall in races, as well as in training, and adjust your speed in practice so that you move closer to the peak of your own performance/speed curve.

Falling Out of Your Mind

Thus far we have suggested exercises for your body in falling. There are also a few things you can do with your mind. First of all, if you are so tense about falling that you cannot attempt the exercises in the previous section or you find that they do not loosen you up, you probably need more formal work on relaxation. In that case, go back to the exercises in chapter 5. Then use a mental image to make falling safer. Rehearse the mental image of yourself falling and not getting hurt, while still being as loose as the Scarecrow.

After the Fall

The above material is designed to prepare your mind for falling. What about after falling? We know some skiers who immediately stand up, look around to see if anyone noticed, and brush themselves off until there is not a flake of snow left on them. These are the people who have not gotten over reason 6, embarrassment. We know other skiers who react to falling by beating the snow with their ski poles while cursing the conditions, their equipment, and themselves. These people are stuck in reason 5—they take their falling as a personal reflection on their ability to ski. Others review in their minds how close they came to really getting hurt, reason 1, thereby traumatizing themselves for the rest of the day. Still others leap to their feet and ski off down the mountain without so much as cleaning the snow off their goggles, as though they were late catching a plane (reason 8).

None of these reactions permits the skier to experience the fall. As a result, nothing is learned and tension is increased. He or she either avoids the experience by pretending it never happened, or distorts it into a physical near-catastrophe or a severe blow to the ego. These reactions are all examples of how not to fall out of our mind. On the other hand, we have some suggestions for how to use your mind after you fall.

Adopt the mental set of being interested in your fall. Before you get up, take a look at how you got there. Review in your mind what happened. What were you thinking, feeling, and doing just before you fell? Were you focused on the sensations in your body and the terrain immediately in front of you, or was your mind all over the place? If concentration was an issue, consider one of our metaphors or create one of your own to hold your attention. How did your body fall? That is, what happened physically to your body? Pay attention to whether you always fall the same way. Is there a pattern to your falling? If so, you may need to make only a minor adjustment in what you're thinking or doing.

Finally, pay attention to what you are saying to yourself after the fall. Are you being critical of yourself or something else? No one and nothing is at fault. *You just fell, that is all.* If you must attach labels to your fall, consider it along positive rather than negative lines. Was it spectacular? Was it the sort of fall that would make a good opening for ABC's "Wide World of Sports"? Was there anything to laugh about? Circus clowns and slapstick comedians make a living out of falling for laughs. Did you make anyone laugh? Most important, did you make yourself laugh? There is a lot of humor in falling. When you fall, keep that image in your mind.

Exercises

1. Review all your reasons for not falling. Consider that they are resistances to experiencing falling, and give yourself permission to fall.
2. Practice falling in the graduated way we described. Repeat this until you can be relaxed about falling.
3. If you have so much tension about falling that practicing does not work for you, spend more time on relaxation and imagery.

    For unplanned falls:

4. Tension check/release. Note whether you are doing a "whew-that-was-close" monologue. If so, stop it.
5. Tension check/release. Review how you got there to see if you have learned anything about what to correct in the future.
6. Tension check/release. Hold the image of a playful child in your mind and allow yourself to experience the humor in your fall.

Getting Stuck on a Horrendous Hill

F irst of all, don't get stuck there if you can help it. Your fear and anger levels are going to be out of control. You will be on the far right side of the performance/arousal curve. *Skiing Out of Your Mind* includes many tactics to desensitize you to high levels of arousal. The relaxation strategies, the self-talk material, shaping your skiing, developing skills in mental rehearsal— all have helped you to center your arousal on the curve.

The problem is that it does not take a great deal to *resensitize* yourself to the ski conditions and terrain that bothered you before. To resensitize is to relearn many of your involuntary emotional responses (in this case, primarily fear and anger) and have those responses influence your skiing and your thinking. Unfortunately, when you resensitize, the problem skiing and the problem thinking generalize past the run you are on and begin to influence your performance on other runs.

So How Did You Get There in the First Place?

We all make mistakes. Sometimes you are not paying attention to the signs. Sometimes you can get talked into skiing a run that ends up looking like a quintuple black diamond and precipitates fear or anger at levels high enough that it feels uncontrollable. On the other hand, some active awareness is also appropriate. Do not just talk yourself out of a challenge when you may need to be challenging yourself. Consider whether the risk-minus-fear equation is reasonably balanced. If it is not balanced, you are resensitizing and setting yourself back. Avoiding this predicament means saying no.

Saying No With Grace

Saying no to skiing companions who ski "out of their minds" is not a problem. Just say no. It should be perfectly understood. Your companions could justifiably ask you to do a little active awareness and discover if you are saying no because you are getting sloppy with your psychology. Under these circumstances they might work with you to help you out. But if that is not the case, and you do not wish to take that run, *say no and don't take it.* Both you and your companions will be comfortable with that.

If your friends have not read this book and are not sensitive to ski psychology but instead keep on pressuring you, you may feel like a kid being called "chicken" in front of your greatest idols. People typically say no by holding someone or something else responsible. They make statements using "you" and "it" instead of "I." Here is a typical dialogue with an inconsiderate ski companion.

"Let's go over to Bellygrabber Pitch."
"Nope. You go. It's not fun."
"Aw, c'mon. It's fun and it's easy enough."
"It's not easy." (Thinking: "It's terrible. Quit pushing me.")
(Determined): "You can do it. I've seen you do the same kind of hill. I'll go slow, for Pete's sake!"
"It's no fun. Go ski the thing if you want to. You're always trying to push me."
"The heck with it. I will. Just go ski your easy hills. Maybe I'll see you at lunch."

We have frequently heard this type of exchange and have sympathized with the victim's feelings of worthlessness and rejection. It is not a pleasant aspect of skiing. Here is an illustration of how "I" statements, and your willingness to take responsibility for your feelings and preferences, can be a way around it.

"*Let's go over and ski Drainpipe.*"
"*Thanks for the invitation, but I prefer to stay here on this run. I'll meet you later if you want.*"
"*Aw, c'mon.*"
"*I really enjoy this run, and I prefer to stay here right now. I would like to meet you in a little while, though.*"
"*You're chicken.*"
"*I can't help it if you think that, but right now I'm enjoying my skiing over here.*"
"*Okay, see you in 30 minutes. Have fun!*"

This latter exchange has a much better ending. Both skiers feel better about each other, their skiing and, most important, themselves.

When You Can't Do it But Have to: P.R.A.Y.!

So you have no choice. You did not say no, or you stumbled onto an unrealistically difficult hill. To you it is a matter of survival: you against the mountain. A double-quintuple black diamond! Your fear is growing. Your mouth is dry. You are thinking, "This is horrible. Just awful. If I don't break something here, it'll be a miracle." You are there, nonetheless. The question now is, how can you use your psychology to (1) get down, and (2) not resensitize yourself with either fear or anger? One thing is for sure. If you keep this up, it is again going to be Mountain—50, Brains—0.

Here is what you should do. It is a straightforward application of tactics you already know. The only difference is that you will be using them at a time when it will seem difficult to get it together enough to even remember them, so we have developed an acronym, appropriately termed for this very situation: P.R.A.Y.

Pause for Several Minutes Stop rehearsing catastrophes. Stop visualizing falls. Stop looking at poor skiers and using them for models. Either look elsewhere or observe and feel with a good skier.

Relax Take a few deep breaths, letting the crisp air into your lungs, feeling calm. Do several tension check/release cycles. You might even include a little negative practice.

Answer Your Disastrous Self-Talk With Coping Self-Statements Some examples: "Okay, I'm here. I can take this a couple of turns at a time. Good." "I have stayed relaxed before. I can do it a couple of turns at a time on this hill, too. It won't feel great, but I'll feel better than I would otherwise have expected." "I do feel more relaxed. This is just what would be expected—that normal tension and stiffening, which is not me. The hill is just more difficult than I'm used to. There, I'm doing fine."

You Mentally rehearse *you* within the skin of a good skier. Visualize and feel that skier. Use body English to enhance the process. Do that every time you pause and relax, *but do not evaluate yourself against that skier*. Use that skier as a model for some calm mental rehearsal.

The net result is that if you are coping, you are not resensitizing. You are doing fine. It may not have been a peak performance, but it will not be long before you can do it—and it will be a peak experience.

Exercises

1. Practice with a friend, or imagine some dialogues in which you use "I" statements to say no with grace.
2. Know the P.R.A.Y. acronym, thinking up a couple of answers (counters) that will work for you. Don't set yourself up to need it, however. That will happen soon enough, and you will be glad to see how effective it is at that time.

CHAPTER 14

Helping
the Minds
of Your Friends

For the most part we have been speaking of skiing as though it were a solitary sport. To be sure, only you are responsible for your skiing. It is your mind and your body that turn your skis or lose your balance. The explanations and exercises we have suggested are for you to do alone so that you can become aware of your own experience. But most people like to ski with someone else. Even if they start the day alone, they are usually happy to meet someone of comparable ability and ski a few turns together. If you are a solitary skier you will not have much use for this chapter. But if you like to ski with other people, we have some thoughts for you.

First of all, if you use the suggestions in this book when you ski, your friends are going to ask such questions as, "Why don't you stop where the rest of us stop anymore? We always stop at the crest of each pitch, but you always ski right over the edge. Has our deodorant failed us or something?" Or they might say, "You've sure been doing some weird things today. Every time we're about to start off down the slope, you say, 'Wait a second,' and close your eyes. What are you doing, anyway? Praying?" If you have not already done so, you might let your friends know what you are doing. Otherwise they may decide that you have finally lost your marbles. We would not want you to lose any friends because you have found some tactics that help you ski better.

In addition to explaining the exercises that you are using for your skiing, there are some things you can do to make *their* skiing more fun. If they are interested in the whole *Skiing Out of Your Mind* approach, we have no objection to your giving them a copy of this book. But we are not suggesting that you proselytize. Don't take a "holier than thou" stance. This is not a belief system or a religious movement. It is merely a series of principles that work, which means that you can make them work for your friends by what you do with your friends.

Being a Model

Skiers learn a lot by observing and imitating each other. However, unless you are a ski instructor you may not feel comfortable modeling ski techniques for your friends. Yet whether you like it or not, you are modeling an attitude toward skiing— a way of thinking, rehearsing, and being on the mountain.

As you know, emotions are contagious. If you are experiencing joy, it will be easier for your friends to be happy with their own skiing. On the other hand, if you are experiencing fear or frustration your friends may pick up on those emotions— unless they know enough to ignore you. Let's assume that they don't. You already know some ways of handling those emotions if they should arise. If you are at the point of coping with your feelings quickly and efficiently, you probably will not be affecting your friends adversely. In fact, they might learn something from observing you. However, if your negative emotions are controlling you instead, you can do your friends a favor by staying away from them temporarily.

Being Your Friends' Best Friend

You can also help your friends when they are having a bad day. What has been your typical reaction to a frustrated friend? Friends usually make one of two responses, neither of which is particularly helpful. One is to be sympathetic and to commiserate.

"Dammit! I can't ski this stuff. I'm so discouraged."

"I know what you mean. You look like you are not doing too well at all. I'm having a terrible time, too. Just look at me. I can't do anything right. I'm skiing as badly as you are. These conditions are terrible."

Misery loves company, right? That's part of the truth. Research in social psychology shows that misery loves *miserable* company. If you truly want to share a friend's misery, you have to become miserable too. Are you ready for that? Even if you do become miserable yourself, you will not be helping your friend. Commiseration does not provide any useful ways of getting out of the misery. In fact, it just reinforces it.

A second common response is to deny the friend's experience altogether by being complimentary:

"Dammit! I can't ski this stuff. I'm so discouraged."

"Gee, I don't see why. You're skiing really well. You look great!"

"No, I don't. Did you see those last turns? I was terrible, awful. Maybe I should quit for the day."

"Oh, no. Don't do that. Honest, you really look good. In fact, you look as good as anyone up here."

"Oh, really?"

This last exchange is particularly insidious. Many skiers have gotten into the habit of berating themselves precisely because they elicit complimentary responses from others. And they usually are unaware that they are using that technique to gain compliments. They do not even know that their friends are unwittingly reinforcing the complaining. Nor do their friends know. Of course, as this pattern is repeated the friends eventually stop being complimentary and stay away from their complaining companion. By then the pattern is well established. Those unfortunate skiers are left with more of their negative self-statements and fewer of their friends.

If you respond to a friend's complaints in either of these two ways, you are not unusual. Nevertheless, it is a problem. Still, this does not mean you should say nothing. That would just turn your friend away. The most constructive things you can say follow from the principles in this book. If your friend is having a bad day and is berating himself or herself, consider a dialogue like the following:

"Dammit! I can't ski this stuff. I'm so discouraged."

"Sounds like you're talking yourself into it. I'd feel pretty discouraged too if I talked to myself like that."

"Well, I just get so frustrated. I can't do anything right. I'll never be a good skier."

"If you say so, you probably won't. You're fighting yourself and your skiing."

"I guess I am, but I can't help myself. The words just came out. I don't know what else to do."

"I have a few suggestions if you don't mind my playing 'teacher.' "

"No, I can use all the help I can get."

"Well, first of all, see what happens if you talk to yourself more realistically. You know it's not that you can't ski this stuff or that you'll never be any good. It's just that you're falling a lot today."

"Yeah, so?"

"So, what's the big deal about falling? That's part of skiing. Everyone falls."

"I guess that's true. But I get so tense when I fall. Then I tighten up and ski miserably."

"And fall some more."

"Right. But what can I do?"

Of course, your dialogue may not go like this one. Your friend may not want to hear your observations at all, or may even want to argue with you as if to convince you that he or she is not any good. In response to that, all you can do is shrug your shoulders and say, "Okay, if you insist that you can't ski, then I guess you can't."

However, if you can arrive at the same point as this dialogue did, with your friend inviting suggestions, you have your foot in the door. From that point, a variety of the tactics in this book could be useful. You might suggest and then model mental rehearsal, or negative practice. Or you might try some shaping tactics as in chapter 8. Whatever tactic you choose *must* be gradual, of course, or neither of you will learn anything. You will become frustrated and your friend will think ski psychology is a crazy notion.

There is one further way that many people have unwittingly become their friends' worst enemy. Typically this occurs when one person knows the terrain ahead and the others do not. The first skier attempts to "help" the others with a few words of warning about the potential catastrophes just around the corner. In trying to forewarn his or her friends of difficulties ahead, this person succeeds only in generating a lot of fear. If it were not a real problem, the dialogue would seem almost comical: "Watch out over the next knoll. It's really rocky and icy. You probably want to take it easy. If you fall, you slide all the way to the bottom. I saw a guy get really scraped up there last weekend. Had to get a toboggan and everything!" With friends like that, who needs enemies? If a friend is going to say anything at all, a more useful comment is: "The next pitch has some ice and rocks in it. I usually find it's best if you stay way over to the right side." Not only does this statement not catastrophize but it also provides some practical information.

Helping Your Friends Toward Active Awareness

As you are aware, there is more to using ski psychology than correcting your friends' self-talk. Your friends probably have not developed much active awareness about their skiing. So if you really want to help them, that is where to start. When they say, "I can't do it," you should ask, "Can't do what? Are you talking about skiing bumps, holding on ice, relaxing, falling, being good to yourself, or what?" In other words, try to help them define the specific problems.

Ask your friend the same questions that you learned to ask yourself in chapter 4 ("Active Awareness"). Your purpose is to *help them refine the reason for their frustration down to something workable.* It is to help them go from amorphous goals like "skiing better" or "having fun" to specifics like "relaxing in the bumps" or "saying nice things to myself, especially when I fall." Once they have distilled their problems down into realistic units, they will be in a better position to use the principles in this book to help themselves. No magic, no mysticism. Just a little psychology.

Do's and Don'ts

- Let your friends know that you are practicing the exercises in this book.
- Share your joy, if that is what you are experiencing.
- Ask your friends' permission if you want to comment on their ski psychology.
- After they fall, make sure they are using the time to covertly rehearse their next few turns and are no longer catastrophizing.
- Help them specify their frustrations into something manageable.
- Notice the differences in your rhythms and respect those differences.
- Be sure to give any specific exercises to your friends in small, manageable steps. That way their success rewards both of you.
- Don't proselytize about this book or its principles. They are neither sacred nor magical.
- Don't be sympathetic, commiserating, or complimentary if your friends berate themselves. You are giving them no new information, only a payoff to continue their complaints.
- Don't share your frustrations if you're being your own worst enemy. Keep your bad feelings to yourself.

CHAPTER 15

Believing and Confidence

Believing. Normally the realm of the theologian, faith healer, spiritualist. But the realm of the sport psychologist? Interesting.

The Power of Belief

February, 1980. The Winter Olympics. There was magic in the air that cold night. Everyone in the small ice-hockey arena could feel it. The crowd was chanting U.S.A.! U.S.A.! U.S.A.! We were going to beat the Russians! The crowd knew it. The youngsters on the team knew it. Some say even the Russians knew it.

E.M. Swift wrote in *Sports Illustrated* of that night: "But the U.S. kids were playing to their potential, perhaps beyond it, and the crowd which had been partially responsible for spurring them to that point, sensed it.... There is nothing quite so idealistic as a young athlete's belief in himself; in a way, the U.S. skaters had so little international experience that they didn't know they weren't good enough to beat the top European teams" (Feb. 28, 1980, p. 26).

Mark Johnson, who had scored two of the four U.S. goals, later told the *New York Times*, "We only had two shots on goal in the second period. But we were only losing 3-2, and that's when we knew we had a chance to win. When we lost to the Russians 10-3 two weeks ago at Madison Square Garden we were down 7-1 after two periods. But being behind by only one goal this time we knew we were younger, we knew we could outskate them, we knew we were going to break our butts to beat 'em. And we did" (Feb. 23, 1980, p. 16).

Of course, not only did they beat the world champion Russian team but they went on to win the gold medal. They did it with more than skill. They believed so strongly in their ability to win that they did.

February, 1984. The Winter Olympics. American skier Bill Johnson was preparing for the Men's Downhill both on the mountain and off. Some of his remarks were quoted in Ski:

"There is basically nothing I can't do right now or at any other time."

"Top three? I'll finish in the top one!"

"I don't know why everybody's here. They might as well hand me the medal now" (Nov. 1984, p. 46).

These comments received a lot of attention, much of it not particularly flattering. Many saw Johnson's belief in himself as rude conceit, no matter how fast his training runs were. It also irritated many of his competitors and perhaps psyched them out in the process. But his belief in himself led him to victory and the gold medal.

Belief is crucial for coaches also. If the coach does not believe in the athlete's ability, chances are the athlete will not do well. You must learn to be your own coach and believe in yourself, and coaches must learn what goes into believing in their athletes.

How does belief work to bring on such peak performance, and how can you get to that level in your own performance? The research in sport psychology that addresses the influence of belief on competitive performance is only beginning to appear. Most of the research on belief has appeared elsewhere, in the areas of clinical psychology, experimental social psychology, and medicine. Let's consider what we can learn from it and see how it applies to skiing.

Most of us have heard of the placebo effect. The word *placebo* derives from the Latin "to please." The placebo effect occurs when a sugar pill works to make us better, as when a person in excruciating pain is told he or she is getting morphine but in fact is not, yet still experiences dramatic relief from the pain. Clinical research shows that a significant number of *us* will respond like that to a placebo! We will get better because of our belief.

It is because of the placebo effect that drug companies use so-called "double blind" studies when they test the effectiveness of pharmaceutical products. A double blind study requires that both the patient (subject) and experimenter be blind to which treatment the subject is receiving, the placebo or the active drug, so that any improvement is due to the actual drug and not the placebo effect. One of the more fascinating things about double blind studies is that even the experimenter cannot know whether he or she is administering the real drug or a placebo, because if the experimenter *believes* the subject is receiving a potentially helpful treatment, this belief can be subtly communicated to the subject and make the subject better. A similar process may occur when a coach believes (or does not believe) in his or her athletes; the coach can make them perform better (or worse).

One of us worked with a coach who communicated a lack of belief. The coach would take each racer aside prior to his or her run and tailor his feedback to that racer, making comments such as, "See that fifth gate? That's just the type of situation you have been having trouble with. Keep that in mind." The kind of mental rehearsal prompted by *that* strategy is obvious! By contrast, a subtle communication of belief and faith might have gone something like this: "See that fifth gate? That's just the type of situation you've been doing so much better in practice with, so you have a good opportunity to use what you know now. Have a great run!"

Faith healing is another example of the effect of belief. Healing by way of the *belief* that the healer has some extraordinary power has been around for millennia. Both the healer and the patient usually believe profoundly and, like the coach and athlete, the relationship between them is especially important.

On the negative side of this are documented cases of illness and death occurring as a result of "curses" placed on the victim—but we know of no documented cases of this occurring when the victim did not *believe* in the power of curses. Similarly, belief may also fail to work for the athlete who has far less belief in himself or herself than does the coach.

Finally, it should be pointed out that healing can work when it is self-generated. That is, belief can influence us even without the "power" of a specific healing person. Journeys to special places believed to have healing powers are an example. In sport, the beliefs of athletes in themselves, in spite of little opportunity to make the team, have resulted in some outstanding performances.

What do we make of all this? Much of it has no generally accepted explanation. Researchers acknowledge the power of believing but their interpretations are varied. However, we know that the relationship between believing and bodily responses is not just magic.

The Changing of Belief

The balance of this chapter ties together the preceding chapters by defining the psychological mechanisms common to changing skiing performance and changing belief. These mechanisms are common to personal change in the broadest sense. This material is more technical than the other material in this book. By including it, we hope to lead you to a better understanding of the learning process you have been through and that which you will encounter as you work toward personal goals.

Given the power of belief and its potential influence on sport performance, it would be ideal to have some easy way to maximize our beliefs, change them as necessary, and ski to our absolute limits. Although changing belief is not a simple task (think about advertising budgets), psychologists are learning more about belief and behavior change. This is especially true of the planned and informed type of personal change that is characteristic of clinical and sport psychology.

What You Believe is What You See

The ancient Stoic philosophers pointed out that we do not respond to an objectively defined world. Instead, *we actively process our world and respond to it as we believe it to be.* You might believe, and see, bumps to be a challenge. You might believe and therefore see chopped powder as your nemesis. You might believe you cannot see at all in flat light, and therefore fail to see anything. You might believe you can (or cannot) win.

New Experience

Although there are many different schools of thought about psychotherapy and behavior change, they all share the requirement of *new experience* as an essential process in the changing of belief. New experience describes precisely what must happen to understand and to change your skiing.

This book has been about new experience. By presenting many ways of changing your skiing and your thinking, our goal has been to inspire you to try out the ideas and to give you success experiences. As you began to recognize that the ideas worked and that you could actually use them while you skied, you increased your belief in both the strategies discussed in this book and in yourself. Your experience showed you that thinking and skiing in certain ways resulted in overall enhancement of your performance. New experience changes your beliefs in yourself and your abilities.

This book also has been about belief: Belief that you could control your thinking. Belief that *if* you controlled your thinking it would help your skiing. Belief that you would be able to move your skis a certain way. Belief that *if* you moved your skis that certain way they would respond as planned. Belief that your success experiences on the mountain would become more frequent and you would learn from them. Belief that you won the race because of your excellent skiing rather than a smooth course or a lucky break in the weather. These types of beliefs pay compound interest. They build upon themselves and lead to belief in yourself. So, just as experience changes your beliefs, beliefs also influence your experience!

What comes first? New experience or new belief? Your *increased ability* to ski or compete well or your *increased belief* in yourself? Perhaps without the experience of thinking and/or skiing in new ways you could not change your belief. Or perhaps without new belief in yourself you could not expand to actually try new skiing skills. If you are serious about your skiing, both are important.

Self-Efficacy: What You Believe You Can Do and What You Believe Will Get the Job Done

Self-efficacy, a scientific theory about belief and belief change, evolved from the research of Stanford University psychologist Dr. Albert Bandura and his associates and was first described by Bandura in 1977.[1] This compelling theory has stimulated a tremendous amount of thought and research by psychologists with interests as varied as academic achievement, sex roles, irrational fears, management of pain, general clinical psychology, and of course sports.

Self-efficacy is made up of two components: *outcome expectations* and *efficacy expectations*.

Outcome Expectations An outcome expectation is defined by Bandura (1977) as "a person's estimate that a given behavior will lead to certain outcomes." Put another way, your outcome expectation is the degree to which you believe that a certain skiing technique or psychological technique will result in a certain outcome (e.g., increased stability or increased speed).

Here are some examples of beliefs about outcomes:

- You believe that the act of holding your hands in front of you rather than dragging a pole will result in the outcome of increased stability as you ski.
- You believe that mental rehearsal will work to help your competitive performance.

The ski technique of "anticipation" is also a good example of outcome expectation, and of how the counterintuitive nature of skiing (recall chapter 1) often throws a wrench in your beliefs about outcomes. In anticipation on steep terrain, the ski behavior we are looking at is moving your upper body ahead of your skis into the center of the new turn. The outcome is increased stability and control. In view of the counterintuitive nature of skiing, this outcome is sometimes difficult to believe: Throwing yourself further down a hill that

---

[1]Bandura, A. (1977). Self-efficacy: Toward a unifying theory of behavioral change. *Psychological Review*, **84**, 191-215.

already feels too steep does not seem to make sense. But it works!

Let's suppose you do give anticipation a try. Suppose further that as you turn your skis into the fall line, you are a little stiff-legged and are placing too much weight on your inside ski. This puts you out of dynamic balance. You sense this imbalance and stiffen even more. You fail to come all the way around, and instead of moving your upper body ahead of your skis you find that your skis shoot out from under you. This causes you to accelerate straight down the hill! You eventually muscle yourself around to a stop, pause with a "Whew!" and begin to review (mentally rehearse) your most recent attempt to anticipate more in your turns on steep terrain. From this it is easy to conclude that the particular skiing behavior called "anticipation" will not in fact give you more control. The net result is that your outcome expectation is low: You do not believe the specific behavior of anticipating in steep terrain results in greater control.

Efficacy Expectations Your outcome expectations do not address the issue of whether you are capable of performing a particular movement or skill on skis. Beliefs about your own capabilities are your efficacy expectations. An efficacy expectation is defined by Bandura as "the conviction that one can produce [a specific] behavior."

To continue with the skiing example of anticipation, let's imagine that you *do* understand and believe that anticipation, when appropriate, *does* result in the desired outcome. You have watched other skiers do this, you understand the mechanics of why it should work, or perhaps you even had one fortuitous turn that demonstrated it to you. Now, to what degree do you believe you are *capable* of doing it? That is your efficacy expectation. As you can see, it is belief about yourself and your behavior. It is your estimate about how capable you are of accomplishing a particular level of performance.

Here are some further examples of efficacy expectations, each of which can vary in the degree to which you actually believe it.

- You believe that you are capable of completing the next 10 turns in the powder between some close trees.

- You believe you can complete a NASTAR race course in your best personal time.
- You believe you will win the 1988 Olympic downhill.
- You believe you are capable of using mental skills.

Efficacy expectations have more influence on future behavior than outcome expectations do, but both are important. For example, if you do not believe you are capable of completing those turns between the trees, your outcome expectations would center on crashing into them. However, it is the changing of efficacy expectations that is the final contribution to enhancement of athletic performance.

You might think of self-efficacy as a scientific view of belief systems and belief change. We do, and we will use the terms "efficacy expectation" and "beliefs" interchangeably. In athletic performance, efficacy and outcome expectations are what is meant by belief. Bandura summarizes this in defining the effect of self-efficacy.[2] Consider your thinking, your skiing, and your living, as you read what he has to say:

Self-percepts of efficacy are not simply inert predictors of future behavior. People's beliefs about their capabilities influence how they behave, their thought patterns, and the emotional reactions they experience in taxing situations. Those who regard themselves as highly efficacious set themselves challenges, intensify their efforts when their performances fall short of their goals, persevere despite repeated failures, make causal ascriptions for failure that support a success orientation, approach potentially threatening tasks nonanxiously, and experience little in the way of stress reactions. Such self-assured endeavor produces accomplishments. *[Emphasis added.] In marked contrast, those who regard themselves as inefficacious shy away from difficult tasks, slacken their efforts and give up readily in the face of difficulties, dwell on their personal deficiencies thus detracting attention from task demands, lower their aspirations, and suffer much anxiety and stress. Self-misgivings undermine performance. Self-percepts of efficacy thus contribute significantly to performance attainments rather than serve merely as forecasters of behaviors to come.* (p. 242)

---

[2]Bandura, A. (1984). Recycling misconceptions of perceived self-efficacy. *Cognitive Therapy and Research*, **8**(3), 231-255.

This is especially relevant for athletic performance:

After capabilities are perfected and massively practiced, perceived self-efficacy is often the difference between a good or a poor showing in athletic contests. This is because with highly perfected skills, a small lapse in effort or accuracy makes a major difference in outcome. (p. 250)

These are the important points we are making about your self-efficacy and how it affects your skiing:

- Your skiing, your thoughts, and your emotions are strongly influenced by your beliefs (efficacy expectations) about your abilities.
- When you believe highly in your ability (high self-efficacy) you challenge yourself, you experience less anxiety, and you try new things more often.
- When you believe highly in your ability but run into the inevitable setbacks, you tend *not* to be your own worst enemy; instead, you keep trying.
- The degree to which you believe in yourself does more than predict that you will ski well. It also contributes to skiing better and better.

As you can see, your belief in your capabilities is crucial to skiing well and to your continuing improvement. Anything you can do to increase your belief about outcomes and efficacy should pay off handsomely. Toward that end, psychologists doing research on self-efficacy have identified four routes to changing your beliefs. We will turn now to those four routes, defining them and explaining how the techniques of *Skiing Out of Your Mind* directly influence both your beliefs and your skiing.

Four Routes to Changing Your Beliefs

The four routes to changing your beliefs are *enactive, cognitive, vicarious, and emotive*.[3] It is not mere coincidence that each route is represented by one or more of the preceding chapters.

---

[3]Strictly speaking, the "cognitive" and "emotive" routes are more properly called "verbal persuasion" and "physiological," respectively. For our purpose here the differences in definition are unimportant.

- You are changing your beliefs by *enactive methods* when you successfully perform some skiing behavior. Enactive methods are presented in chapter 8 on using operant techniques to enhance your performance. Examples include the techniques of shaping better skiing by working up to the problem, and interrupting problem triggers by keeping your rhythm as you ski over the edge of steeper pitches.

- You are changing your beliefs by *cognitive methods* when you use your mind whether on or off the mountain. Cognitive methods include imagery, constructive thinking, concentration, and metaphors and are covered in chapters 6, 9, 10, and 11, respectively.

- You are changing your beliefs by *vicarious methods* when you learn by looking (chapter 7). Observing other skiers, whether better or worse, teaches a great deal both about outcomes and efficacy.

- You are changing your beliefs by *emotive methods* when you use relaxation (chapter 5) and/or imagery (chapter 6) to center your emotional arousal for maximum performance as illustrated by the performance/arousal curve.

These are the purest examples, but these routes do not operate independently. However, each of them individually or in combination provides the essential foundation for increasing your belief and confidence. Let's look at this foundation in more detail.

Enactive Routes You are approaching a field of unbroken powder. Perhaps you feel only 30% confident about skiing it well. You push off and are pleasantly surprised to find you are making some of your turns very well. Your confidence grows a bit, and you push over the next pitch. Your instructor then points out a different way to shift your weight. You try (perform) it, find that it works better, and try it again. You continue throughout the day with the ups and downs so typical of skiing. The next morning you are greeted with 11 new inches of crystalline powder as you approach the same run. If asked to rate how strongly you believe you could make even more of your turns well, you would probably rate the likelihood higher than the previous day. You have changed your beliefs. You have done so through the performance accomplishments that are the core of the enactive routes to belief change.

Here are further performance-based (enactive) examples from chapter 8. Each leads to belief change:

- You lose your balance and nearly fall, but you do not stop with a "Whew, that was close!" Instead, you continue to ski until you recover and stop from a position of strength. As you become more adept at regaining your balance, your efficacy expectations include the belief that you are increasingly capable of making recoveries.
- You begin to shape better skiing by trying a few turns in and out of the chopped snow on the sides of runs. Your beliefs about your capability to ski this kind of snow increases as you build up success experiences.

Prior to the 1985 World Cup Slalom in Maribor, American racer Tamara McKinney was fifth after the first run of the women's slalom. She went all out on the second run and won the event. In a television interview afterward, her comments on how she felt about winning illustrated how important a performance accomplishment is for efficacy expectations. She told the interviewer, "I needed something to put in my confidence pocket." What a nice phrase!

Enactive methods are a primary route to belief change in skiing, and they make good common sense. As you become more successful in your skiing, you will *believe* differently. This is also true of other things in life; your *performance accomplishments* are a critical source of information about your capabilities. With performance accomplishments, your efficacy expectations change. In other words, your belief in yourself changes.

Where enactive routes to belief change rely on new behaviors that lead to new accomplishments, the other routes are more subtle. Recall that you do not actually have to perform a particular skiing behavior in order to change your belief. Examples include the mental techniques of imagery, vicarious learning, metaphors, modification of self-talk, or changing your standard-setting. These do not require that you ski to be able to effect significant belief change. The cognitive, vicarious, and emotive routes thus have the advantage of being useful on or off the mountain. This is where efficacy theory really shines. It explains how you can begin to change your beliefs even without performing the skill in question. To wire-in a new belief, however, you will need to experience performance accomplishments eventually.

Cognitive Routes   We categorize constructive thinking, concentration, metaphors, and imagery as cognitive routes to belief change. To this we should add the effect that an instructor, friend, or coach might have on your thinking and your ski performance as he or she provides a source of support and verbal persuasion about your capabilities. The power of suggestion also begins on a cognitive route, whether the suggestion is a change in diet or a statement of belief in sport psychology.

There is a strong cognitive part in each of the four routes to belief change. This is most obviously true of the interdependence of the cognitive and enactive routes. As you find yourself having new and successful experiences on skis, you attach labels to yourself and your skiing. Examples of these thoughts (or cognitions) would be, "Wow! I did do that with some grace!" or "I sure do look forward to another day of powder this deep...I'm finally getting it."

In these examples, your positive thoughts have *followed* your performance accomplishments and were carried forward with you into new situations. This is great, but it differs a bit from the direct use of the cognitive route to *lead you* to your skiing accomplishments. The power of the cognitive route to lead you to new horizons is found in its use prior to the successful performance. That is, the power is in the ability of the cognitive route to prepare you to try new things and interpret your victories (and setbacks) appropriately. Chapter 9 on constructive thinking is one of the best illustrations of that point, as well as the material in chapter 3 on self-criticism, self-punishment, and standard-setting.

Here is a brief case example of using the cognitive route to lead you to increased performance:

You worry obsessively about blowing a difficult gate in an important race. Although you are quite sure you can complete the race, you worry that if you press hard enough to have a winning time you may not be able to stay on course through that gate. Now, in the process of worrying, you are increasing your tension levels and mentally rehearsing your anticipated poor performance.

Using the cognitive route to belief change, you would relabel the situation with statements such as, "I have had difficult gates in the past and they didn't slow me to last place" or "Here is what I have to do to hit those gates right" (use appropriate imagery at this point).

In this example, your labels competed with the tension and you increased your rehearsal of competent imagery. You should then be able to shift your efficacy expectations enough to improve your performance. Assuming you do not discount your accomplishment, you will likely cope in a similar fashion in future races.

Vicarious Routes   Learning by looking, the subject of chapter 7, provides another way of gaining information about efficacy. You gain information about the emotional responses of the model (e.g., powder can be skied in a relaxed manner) and about the physical capabilities required to execute the turns through that field of powder. You also gain information about outcomes. For example, by observing the repeated successful outcomes of using anticipation on steep terrain you will increase your outcome expectations.

When you are on skis and actively involved with your coach or instructor, you are combining vicarious routes with performance accomplishments. Called "participant modeling," it is an excellent way to change both efficacy and outcome expectations. You get the opportunity to watch, create appropriate imagery, try the skill, and then get feedback.

Your friends can also help enhance your beliefs, if you will let them. This is part of the process of psyching up. Listening to other skiers model efficacy and listening to them hoot and howl as all of you are floating down that field of powder or carving elegant lines through the moguls is a powerful shared experience.

Employing the vicarious route to gain information about efficacy and applying it to the same case example of the difficult gate would go like this:

You worry obsessively about that difficult gate. To attack this problem through the vicarious route, you must shift your attention to each competitor as he or she approaches the start. You focus on their concentration and watch their positioning and their apparent single-mindedness as they look down the course. You mentally place yourself at the start, using body English as the skier presses onto the course. You watch the complete run (or use imagery if that is not possible), focusing on continuity.

By using this strategy to block competing thoughts, that is, by actively observing another skier and "experiencing" the turns that skier is making, you should be able to shift your perceived self-efficacy. As that shift occurs, your performance will improve. As you discover that your performance improves, you will continue to use this approach in future races.

Emotive Routes Chapters 4, 5, and 6, dealing with active awareness of your arousal levels, learning relaxation techniques, and learning to use imagery to center your arousal, demonstrate how critical your arousal levels are to your skiing. This is especially true of competitive performance. Recall that the performance/arousal curve illustrates that there is an optimal level of arousal for each of us.

Emotional arousal affects your beliefs in a variety of ways. First, your arousal level influences the way you process and mentally rehearse information. For example, when your arousal is experienced as anxiety, you will see and rehearse the ski run ahead as frightening and your capabilities as minimal. You might see (focus on) several large moguls, wondering (negatively rehearsing) how they might throw you. Your performance further suffers because of excess physical tension, and you confirm by several tense failures that you are not capable of skiing that run. Eventually, even your recollection of the run will be distorted by your high arousal, as will your evaluations of your future performances. Thus, excessive arousal has led directly to lowered self-efficacy.

Researchers have addressed another way that your arousal level affects your beliefs. It appears that high arousal levels can trigger both imagery and cognitions. When your arousal is very high, failure imagery and thoughts may be significantly increased from the outset. As you become aware of those thoughts, your belief in your capabilities will be low. High arousal has led to perceptions of low self-efficacy that may be confirmed in a future performance failure. Thus, emotions offer much information about your perceived capabilities— your belief in yourself.

The negative practice technique in chapter 5 is a way of altering such a cycle. The goal is to increase awareness of high arousal levels so that they can be handled before the cycle begins. As you gain from this and lead yourself to some performance accomplishments to wire-in the gains, you have used the emotive route to change belief in yourself. Relaxation techniques that significantly reduce arousal also increase performance accomplishments.

There is one important point to add about the emotional experience of anxiety and your efficacy expectations. According to efficacy theory, your estimates of efficacy do not include comment on how anxious you may be *while* skiing or performing some other behavior. By definition, it simply asks whether or not you think you can execute the behavior, and then asks you to rate how confident you are that you can in fact accomplish it. In other words, you are not asked, "How nervous will you be when you ski that steep field of powder?" Instead, you are asked whether you can do it and how *confident* you are that you can do it. Ultimately it matters little whether you experience anxiety or not, according to efficacy theory; what matters is the degree to which you believe you can perform regardless of anxiety. Although your anxiety level while performing is not included as part of your efficacy expectation, your personal anticipation of anxiety may certainly have influenced your confidence ratings.

Rituals and Belief

Most competitors have a precompetition ritual. Some rituals make sense but others appear more like superstition. For example, a ritual for preparing equipment and dressing seems to make sense on the face of it (it has what psychologists call "face validity"), but a ritual about a lucky charm or particular piece of clothing seems more typical of superstition. However, the fact is there are sound reasons why rituals of any sort work well for many athletes. First, they set the stage for maximizing efficacy expectations, and second, they set the stage for minimizing the rehearsal of self-defeating thoughts and images. Rituals thus can be thought of as a set of procedures, bolstered by faith, that are valuable because they set you up for several kinds of productive psychological work.

- Rituals help in the recollection of past successful performances. The use of a ritual makes you feel positive largely because you have usually associated it with past successful performances. It matters less what kind of ritual it is than how well it seems to work. This is because in the process of recalling your past performance accomplishments you are mentally rehearsing your competence. As the ritual is rewarded, you will increase the consistency of its use and of the associated thoughts about your abilities.

- Rituals often initiate a problem-solving mode of thinking. They are valuable because they give you time to think about and mentally "solve" problems in advance. Examples include difficult snow conditions or a difficult gate placement. This is especially true of those rituals that occupy time prior to a competition, such as equipment preparation.

- Rituals help reduce the frequency of thoughts that compete with optimum performance both directly and indirectly. They do so directly because it is often preoccupying to be involved in your ritual. They do so indirectly because the presence of appropriate mental rehearsal (as pointed out above) displaces self-defeating imagery.

- Like Linus' blanket, rituals can make your environment more familiar, safe, and comfortable. When faced with new physical environments (e.g., new hotel or dressing facilities, new locales for competition), ritual gives you an opportunity to standardize what occurs prior to your performance. You carry your ritual with you and its use enables you to lower the impact of distraction.

There is one caution about rituals. As you will see in the next few paragraphs, taking credit for your accomplishments has an important impact on your beliefs. If your ritual is strictly of the lucky charm type, you must monitor how you interpret your athletic performance. If you believe that the charm *caused* a high performance, you will be in trouble if it starts failing. On the other hand, if you attribute your success to your own increasing physical and psychological skills (even if aided by your ritual), you will be more likely to carry that forward into future performances.

Responsibility

When we talk about responsibility in a book on sport psychology, we are not talking about responsibility for your parents, spouse, children, sister, brother, or ski instructor. We are talking about *you* taking responsibility for your personal changes in your thinking and skiing. Look how easy it is to discount what would seem to be, and should be, positive new experiences:

- "I would never have made it down that run without my ski instructor along!"
- "Heck, the course was perfect and the light was brilliant. I could have turned in the same time yesterday under those conditions."
- "I don't think practicing these mental skills works at all. I just made up my mind I would stay in that line through the bumps and got lucky."
- "My lucky charm worked again!"

Belief in yourself means believing you are responsible for your new experiences of thinking and skiing. By contrast, if you are unable to attribute your positive gains to your own endeavor, you are setting yourself back. When you place responsibility elsewhere for positive events in your skiing or your life, your belief in your own capability will grow slowly if at all.

Sometimes it is appropriate to place the responsibility for an unsatisfying performance elsewhere. Belief in yourself also means knowing when to realistically do that. This is much better than condemning yourself inappropriately and lowering your efficacy expectations, which is one way that being your own worst enemy works to lower your belief in your capabilities.

The process of changing belief thus requires a step beyond the use of the four routes to changing efficacy expectations. It must also include accepting appropriate responsibility for your performance. That is, it must be thought about, processed, and "owned" as something *you* are doing.

Often a lack of accepting responsibility is due to thoughtlessness; it is not a conscious effort. If you have an experience that does not match your concept of yourself, you usually do not even think to "own" it. In fact, it is often difficult to "see" it. Considering that the extraordinary effect of your beliefs even extends to how you process the information that your world presents to you, it is as if you had filters on your senses that only let in information that fits. Here are some examples:

- If you are not a racer and turn in a poor time on a NASTAR course, you are unlikely to put yourself down as a poor racer. This is because the realization that you are not a racer lets you accept the evidence at face value.
- On the other hand, if you are a recreational racer and you turn in a record-setting time that does not match your concept of yourself, you are likely to attribute it to luck or some other external cause. Again, this is because you have scarcely looked at the evidence but instead decided in favor of what "fits." Unfortunately, when you think like that you gain little benefit from that positive experience.

Much of changing belief, then, is increasing your ability to own your skiing, making the *positive* changes fit like a warm glove. When in skiing (and in life) it is the negative that fits like the warm glove, the price of that fit is high. Even your positive experiences will have little impact in your quest for personal growth. Your journey will be a long one.

...And Make Your Belief Happen

Do not be discouraged by the reality that believing in yourself takes work! Skiing well takes work. Living takes work. We suspect that Bill Johnson's beliefs did not just pop into his mind. Neither did those of the Olympic hockey team. Nor do our beliefs in ourselves pop into our minds. They are earned!

Think about the obstacles overcome in the process of changing belief and developing confidence: *Anxiety*...but you calm yourself to try for the first time. *Self-doubt*...but you talk constructively to yourself enough to allow you to try a new experience. *Pain*...but you label it differently, or mentally distract yourself as you press on. *Brooding*...but you practice realistic evaluations of your ability and use your accomplishments to build upon. *Comparisons* with the ever-present "better skier"...but you use his or her energy and skill to provide you an image rather than a discouragement. *Losing*...but you use the momentum and the emotion of the winner as part of your dream.

This is what belief change and confidence is about. In athletics, and in our lives, it does not just happen. With all that you have learned, *you make it happen.*

Transcendence

P R.A.Y.ing . . . relaxing . . . rehearsing . . . your music . . . your metaphors . . . your rhythm . . . your
falls . . . your friends . . . your own
worst enemy . . . your own best friend . . . your S.E.L.F. . . . from
out of your mind. How does it all fit together? There is a right-
brain and a left-brain answer to that.

First, the linear, logical, left-brain answer: Using the scientific approach to active awareness, you identified your
strengths and weaknesses and set some specific objectives for
improvement. It wasn't magic, and it wasn't mysticism. Working with the tactics in this book, you approached your problems positively and systematically. You relaxed, you coped
with your frustrations, you dealt with your anger, and you
found that the work of *Skiing Out of Your Mind* was fun. So
you extended yourself, seeking new personal challenges. You
played with images and rhythms. You improved your concentration. You discovered two of your own best friends: you and
the mountain. The challenge remains. You continue to improve, and you find joy in doing one thing better today than
you did yesterday. You take satisfaction in using your mind
and your sense of self-efficacy increases.

Now the holistic, experiential, right-brain answer: You pur-
sued the suggestions in this book and experienced the joy of
improvement. Then one day you find you are skiing without
thinking about tactics, or anything else for that matter. You
are totally immersed. Nothing exists except the sense of grace,
of oneness with the mountain, and a single clear note ringing
in your head. In a letter to his long-time skiing friend Charles

Lobitz, the Canadian poet Claude Liman wrote of a peak experience, of his awareness of . . .

my brother's exquisite motion down the slope; I push off and follow in his wake, beneath the double chair where people are still leaning out to admire how he goes. Suddenly I am young again and the people are leaning out to watch me, too. There is sun on a wide expanse of trail, all of it flowing downhill with me riding it like a chip in a current. I don't really have to move. Motion is around me, and I am carried. Moguls are waves which can only be negotiated by instinct, by launching oneself into the pattern and learning the maze by sheer reaction. I do not turn so much as push off each ledge, then the next and the next, reversing when the ground comes up to be a platform for my next impulse. I never could make good turns on slopes the snowcats have groomed into boredom. I must feel I am unlocking a mystery with each reaction to minute pieces of new terrain. Certain runs have that inevitable quality of destiny, when sunlight and snow and air and me and a path through the moguls intersect at that auspicious moment. Motion is the catalyst.

You finish the run in a state of ecstasy: "My God, that was incredible!" When you return home, you think back through this book, trying to recall the chapter on that experience. You would like to make it happen again.

But the chapter doesn't exist. It doesn't work that way. All of the systematic exercises, all of the work, and all of the fun of *Skiing Out of Your Mind* came together in that one beautiful moment. At that point—a point in space, perhaps, or time—there was an intangible merging of thinking and experiencing.

So you go back to working on your challenges, taking satisfaction in using your mind and knowing that the experience will come again. You go back to the end of chapter 1 . . .

to let go, to feel, to be aware of your relationship with the mountain in space and time. It fits together as an entire experience, a gestalt, an integration of your body and mind that, when working right, seems spiritual in its beauty and grace. It is an intense individual challenge, a communication between a lone skier and a mountain that is itself as complex in variety as you are in your feelings and thoughts and ways of skiing.

Further Thoughts for Instructors

Teaching Mental Skills

I t is easy to introduce the *mind* as an aid to your students' skiing. In our cerebral society, most of us welcome the opportunity to think about something, even on ski slopes. This is especially true of the people who have paid money to learn something new. If you tell your students that you are going to help them use their minds as well as their bodies to improve their performance, very few will object. For those who do, as soon as they understand what you are asking them to do and why, the barriers will usually come down. Much depends on you. If you approach the mental skills training with the same enthusiasm and style as you do the motor skills, the students will be equally enthusiastic. This is the essence of vicarious learning.

Throughout this book you have read many examples of mental techniques you can adapt to your ski classes. In addition, there are specific situations in which these psychological principles can be particularly helpful. In this appendix we make some additional suggestions for teaching mental skills and dealing with mental barriers. These suggestions are organized according to the chapters of the book. We have done this so that if you have any questions on when and where to apply these tactics, or how they may work, you can refer back to the original chapter. These suggestions stem from our experience as ski instructors and psychologists, and they have proven useful in helping students take control of their own skiing.

One concept that is central to teaching mental skills is consistency. Mental skills are difficult for the average skier to believe in. The results are not as immediately apparent as are the results of a successfully executed technical pointer. If mental skills are not used consistently, little is learned about how best to use them, they are not very rewarding when haphazardly applied on the mountain, and their benefit is minimal. Part of your job, then, is to *model* their consistent use. Let your students watch you use mental rehearsal before demonstrations. Let them see you use body English as you are learning by looking. Let them hear you be good to yourself, and to them, as you use constructive thinking. The conscientious use of mental skills should become as much a part of skiing as the conscientious use of technique.

A second general concept to remember is that mental skills can be tailored to the needs of individual students just as you emphasize different technical pointers to different students. There is not one big "mental skill" that is applied to all problems. Rather, it is more like assessing the problem and reaching onto the shelf to pull down the right ingredients for a prescription. For example, one student may benefit most from learning how to modify runaway self-criticism, another by learning to center his or her arousal (especially anxiety), a third by learning to use previsualization, and so forth. As you use *your* active awareness to analyze students' problems, you are doing two things: You are modeling how to use active awareness, and you are modeling the point that the best approach to using mental skills is to tailor them according to need.

Be creative! We believe you already have many useful tactics of your own, and we hope you might find some new ones here to add to your repertoire.

1—Psychology and Skiing

Mind Reading

Try to avoid mind reading. Just because a person appears tense to you does not mean he or she is scared. This person could be angry, cold, or even unaware of any tension-producing thought or image. Instead of guessing, ask what thoughts and images such individuals are experiencing. Discover what they believe about themselves and their skiing. Cultivate your active awareness—and theirs—by asking "what" questions rather than "why" questions. For example, instead of "Why are you tense?" try "You appear tense. What are you thinking?" The former question invites speculation on the part of a student you already know is naive in the use of mental skills; the latter yields good information and also models the development of active awareness.

2—It's Frightening What Fear Does to Your Skiing

First Aid for Panic

If you have ever had a student panic on a lift, you know how serious a problem it is—not only for that student but for the rest of the class as well. Sometimes you could swear fear is contagious. (Psychologically it is, as explained in chapter 7.) With a class of novice skiers, panic can almost be an epidemic. It differs from fear and anxiety in that the panicked person is at the limit of control. The most important thing for you to do is to keep this person from going over the edge. There are probably as many ways of doing this as there are instructors. The following is one we have found to be effective.

That first lift ride for many new skiers can be frightening. One of the reasons for introducing the relaxation process to never-evers is that if you are faced with such a situation, you will have a basis from which to work. You can often get a hint of the likelihood of some students to panic if you ask them to rate on a 1-10 scale how anxious they are about riding the lift. Make a habit of riding the lift with the person who reports the highest anxiety rating.

If panic occurs, it usually includes an almost irresistible urge to flee. But from 30 feet up on a lift that is impossible. The person is caught in an awful internal conflict and is literally on the brink of jumping. He or she wants to get out of there but cannot. It is an impossible situation, like being caught between a rock and a hard place.

Outwardly, the person may be hyperventilating, perhaps shaking, and pleading for help. Unless you have experienced it yourself, it is very difficult to imagine how overwhelming this situation can be.

Handle it by being a relaxed model, projecting your voice calmly and with authority. Make physical contact. Have him or her hold your hand if possible. Sometimes a panic-stricken student will find it difficult to let go of whatever he or she is gripping. In that case, get a strong grip on the student's arm or hand.

Assign something to do. In a calm, strong voice, give directions such as, "Take a deep breath and hold it. Good. Now as you hold it, tense your entire body. Good." Continue talking calmly, "Now let the air out of your lungs, and as you do, let go of as much tension as you can." At this point, if you are holding a hand or arm, gradually lighten your grip in synchrony with the student's exhalation. Do a tension-release cycle several times and say "See, you do have control of your muscles." It is important to point this out, since people in such circumstances are fighting for control, and any sense of control can ease the panic. In addition, you are giving them something they can do to control themselves.

Continue talking calmly, going through several more cycles of synchronizing the strength of your grip with their tension-relaxation sequence. It is ideal if you can observe and encourage tension-relaxation of the leg muscles at the same time. Toes curling downward in the boots or tension-relaxation of the quadriceps will do fine.

As you approach the unloading ramp, have your student take a deep breath and hold it, and as the two of you stand up, have him or her exhale. More than likely the unloading will proceed uneventfully.

Textbook Explanations

This chapter has been long on explanation of what fear does to skiing. We have found that some students respond particularly well to this type of intellectual understanding of "why" they could benefit by using certain mental skills (e.g., lowering tension or changing self-talk). Others do not. We suggest you tailor this type of explanation to the student, perhaps going into some detail on the lift as appropriate. That student will appreciate it, and the others will be spared a lecture on a windy mountain.

3—On Being Your Own Worst Enemy

Back-Talk

When a student begins the "I'm not any good" monologue, you can demonstrate just how those words affect physiology by throwing them right back at the student. *Ask permission* to demonstrate what he or she is doing, and then yell "You're not any good!" several times. Then ask about the student's response to those words. Most people will express anger, embarrassment, or some other negative reaction. You can now point out that their physiology cannot easily distinguish between your words and their own self-talk, and that their performance and learning suffer because of it. They are being their own worst enemy.

When they understand the effect this has on them, offer the tactic of relabeling with specific examples such as those illustrated in chapter 9 on changing self-talk. Listen to two or three brief suggestions of their own for new labels, and rehearse them in the relabeling technique several times. Continue to be aware of how they are doing with it as the lesson proceeds.

One variation of this exercise is to let the class observe your back-talk and to explain why you are doing it. Again, be very careful to get the students' permission before back-talking to avoid unexpected embarrassment.

4—Active Awareness and Being Your Own Personal Scientist

Kinesthetic Awareness for Never-Evers and Seldom-Evers

For never-evers, the rotary movements of the legs are strange and difficult to do. One way you can enhance the learning and awareness of these movements is by giving them a little physical therapy. This is how it is done.

1. Kneel beside your student. Grasp the right foot, heel in one hand, top of toes in the other. Instruct him or her to keep the right leg relaxed, rotate the foot, toes in, heel out. Repeat this several times with each foot, keeping the leg relaxed.
2. Have your student help you by gradually moving one leg, being sure to keep the rest of the body quiet and relaxed. If you find his or her arms or other leg moving, it is probably due to pushing too hard. Have him/her ease up some.
3. When your student can rotate one leg comfortably without help and with little or no other body movement, begin to *resist* the movements, gradually increasing the resistance for each foot until it becomes necessary to use considerable muscle power. When this can be accomplished with the rest of the body relaxed, you have begun to program this movement into the neuromuscular system.

If you haven't done this with students, you might want to give it a try. It's interesting how weak the first few rotations are, and even more interesting how strong they get after the wedge is established in their skiing.

Clues to Cues

On the first lift ride, have your students think about the last great run they had. Ask them to make a mental note of the external environment, such as weather, type of snow, and terrain. Then ask them to recall their internal environment, that is, emotions they were experiencing, any thoughts and/or images they can recall, and what their movements felt like.

On another lift ride, have them go through the same procedure for their last awful run. Often this will be much more detailed than the good one. Have them compare the two for differences and similarities. You and they now have two sets of information from which to set the stage for change.

The Response Systems and Desynchrony

Recall the three response systems discussed in this chapter: the cognitive, behavioral, and physiological. It is interesting that the experience of emotional arousal is often quite different for different people, even though they would use the same label to describe it.

Take the label "anxiety" as an example. In terms of the relative contribution of each of the response systems to the *experience* of anxiety, each of us is quite different. You may find students who are cognitively fearful, reporting many anxiety images or self-statements but low physiological arousal. Their heart rate is not particularly high, nor do they appear particularly tense, but they talk as if they are indeed quite anxious. Alternatively, students may report little by way of cognitive events and little avoidance behavior, but still look extremely tense to you as they ski.

This phenomenon is called *desynchrony* of the response systems. It is important to be aware of this because it enables you to suggest the appropriate mental skills for each student. This should remind you that active awareness is the first step in tailoring mental skills training to a student's needs. You are modeling the process of active awareness. You are also modeling the necessity of using mental skills prescriptively rather than in a shotgun approach which leads to inconsistency, lack of believability, and especially lack of fun!

5—Relaxation: Body and Mind

Never-Evers: Prime Time to Introduce Relaxation

If you introduce relaxation to new skiers, they are likely to make it a routine part of their skiing, just as stretching and warm-up are a routine part of yours. Here is one way you can do this:

Pick an isolated place, on a flat, where there will be as little distraction as possible. It should be one of the first things you do with your group. Have the group stand, eyes closed, in a circle with you in the middle. You will draw attention to the contrast between tense and relaxed states. Have them take a deep breath, hold for a count of two, exhale. Direct them to gradually tense and then release: hands, forearms; jaw, neck; shoulder shrugs, droops; knees locked, unlocked; toes curled, uncurled. Finish with another deep breath, suggest a whole body tension check, and release as they exhale. When giving the directions, use a calm voice, paced fairly slowly. The entire sequence takes about 5 minutes, including a short explanation.

Go on to whatever you do at the start of your lesson. Periodically throughout the class take a few moments to do a tension check/release. Suggest that the students begin to do this on their own.

Anchor Relaxation to the Scenery

With beginners you usually take a few breaks, so make one of these a relaxation break. To help establish the tension check/release as part of their skiing, have the students look at the scenery immediately before and after the routine. They can use the beauty of the scenery as a reminder to do their tension check/release.

Of course this relaxation sequence need not be reserved only for beginners. It can and should be used for any level. We believe, however, that it is more likely to become a fixed part of the skier's repertoire if it is introduced right at the beginning of his/her skiing experiences.

For more advanced skiers, the Tin Man/Scarecrow exercises in chapter 5 are useful and fun.

Relaxation on the Lift

Since your students are more than likely to be in pairs, have one lead the relaxation sequence for the other while riding the lift. If the lift is long enough they can switch roles. The important point here is that you should direct their use of lift time. Many students do not even perceive lift time as useful for self-directing mental skills to enhance their ski performance, so now is an ideal time to begin that habit.

6—Mental Imagery and Mental Rehearsal

Lift Assignments

Give your students practice at mental rehearsal. Begin by having them rehearse something they are already doing well on skis. Then you can ask them to rehearse a new skiing strategy, such as finishing turns with a crunch or letting the skis float into the fall line. After a great run or even one good turn, have them replay it immediately in their minds after the run so that replay during lift time is facilitated. Following are exercises you can assign that will help in developing your students' visual and kinesthetic imagery:

1.   Have your students focus on the chair in front of them, closing their eyes for longer and longer periods and "seeing" that chair in their mind's eye.
2.   With eyes closed, have your students move their feet several inches apart and then open their eyes to see how far apart they really are. Have them do this several times, varying the distance each time.
3.   Have your students rotate their feet, watching and feeling the movements. Have them close their eyes and picture their skis moving as they feel themselves rotate their feet. Have them try to keep their skis parallel when doing this, opening their eyes from time to time for visual feedback.
4.   Repeat #3, but this time with their eyes closed have them gently stop moving their feet, relaxing them and letting the rotary movement gradually stop. Have them mentally continue these movements, extending them into the future, after they have stopped actual movement.

7—Vicarious Learning: Learning by Looking

Modeling Mental Skills

As instructors, you know the importance of presenting a clear, precise model of the skill you are teaching. This is true whether you are modeling a motor skill or a mental skill. As we pointed out earlier, if you choose to teach such skills as previsualization, constructive self-talk, and relaxation, practice what you preach! To do otherwise makes a mockery of an aspect of skiing that is difficult to learn and practice to begin with. Because it reduces the believability of mental skills training, you are laying the groundwork for a "mindless" skier.

Modeling as Feedback

There are times when words fail, as for example when you feel you need to point out a constant error but don't want to harp. In this case you can mimic your student's error. This sounds like heresy, but it is a type of vicarious negative practice. You mimic the error, *but do not stop there*. Move from the error to the correct movements. You are literally giving a picture of where your student is, and where he or she should aim. Additionally, the last image you leave with the student is the one you want him or her to capture. By giving the student this picture, you also give a strong sense of identification with you. Once this is established, he/she can keep that identification as you continue to shape the more appropriate behavior. The stronger the identification, the more effective the modeling.

Use of Imagery

When you give a demonstration, you want it to be as efficient as possible. You can increase its efficiency if you give a few clear directions to your students on how to watch. Start by asking them to watch only the demo. They should not attend to other skiers until you have taught them how to pick a model as discussed in this chapter. When the stage has been set, proceed as follows:

1. Teach (and model) how to watch with body English as set forth in this chapter.
2. Teach them to then close their eyes and replay the image/feeling in their mind.
3. They are then to open their eyes and ski to that image.
4. After completing the run, they should begin the process of wiring-in the past by mentally rehearsing what they just did.

Be sure to observe your students as the day goes on so you can reinforce their continued use of mental rehearsal. As you see one or more students doing this, point it out to the class with encouragement to continue.

The exercise discussed later in which you take a beginner to a "cliff" provides a fine opportunity to begin teaching how to find a model and how to look. When you observe that your students are able to look over the steeper pitch and stay calm, have them look for skilled skiers on the slope. Point out appropriate models if available, and have them watch with body English. Instruct them to carry the image into the future by closing their eyes momentarily and feeling as if they are within the skin of that good skier.

Use and Misuse of Video

Because of the power of modeling, videotapes can enhance a student's learning. However, that power can also be used destructively. Many people have a negative idea of how they look. When they see themselves, they will tend to filter what they see and support their belief by focusing on their errors rather than on their accomplishments. If you add to that by pointing out their errors, you will be reinforcing the very thing you want to let lapse. The students are more likely to remember those things you point out, and since they are seeing themselves the reinforcement is very strong.

Elicit comments from the students by using phrases like, "Tell me what you see." When the students tell you what they are seeing, they are telling you what is important to them and what their beliefs about their skiing are. Make sure you emphasize the positive. Search for skiing that *competes* with the errors the students may be observing. Whenever *you* see something you want remembered and reinforced, tell them what you see and add a reinforcing phrase.

To end the session, make sure the students are left with a positive image. A good way of assuring this is for you to ski last during the taping session. Additionally, we have found it helpful to have a separate tape of ourselves or others providing a good model; we end the session by showing that tape.

In summary, when using video:

1. Ask students to tell you what they are seeing.
2. Give reinforcement for correct or nearly correct moves.
3. Leave the student with a final image of the appropriate skiing.

8—Enhancing Performance With Operant Techniques

Feedback as a Shaping Tool

Feedback is Reinforcing   In giving feedback, you call attention to what the student is doing. As a result you increase the chance that the student will remember it and subsequently use mental rehearsal. Thus if you give feedback on something the student is doing *wrong*, that is what the student is more likely to remember. Be thoughtful about what you call attention to with your feedback. Be sure to offer suggestions that *compete* with the mistakes so the mistakes are not maintained. For example, relaxation competes with tension; realistic goals compete with self-punishment, and so forth.

When to Give Feedback   When you see your student either doing the thing you are working on or doing something similar, describe to him or her what you are seeing. You might wish to add a reinforcing phrase.

When Not to Give Feedback   When your student is apparently focused on what he or she is doing, and thus is providing his or her own feedback, why interrupt this valuable process with words of your own? That would only be distracting. Save the feedback for the conclusion of the movement or run.

9—Constructive Thinking: Changing Your Self-Talk

Stop! That Old Habit

We often find that students will perform the specific new skill we are teaching as long as we lead them or make it part of an exercise series. As soon as we ask them to incorporate that skill into their free skiing, however, they often revert back to the old habit. We know that each time they return to the old habit it gets further reinforced, so it is important that they learn to stop it. And that is just what you can do. Use a variation of the thought-stopping technique. Tell the student that whenever you see him/her skiing the old way, you will yell "Stop!" and you want him or her to stop skiing. You then direct him/her to mentally rehearse the specific new skill and then to start again.

Do this as often as necessary, encouraging the student to learn to do it on his/her own. One word of caution: Recall that when a skier stops because he or she is out of control or is making an error, this sometimes ushers in a monologue of self-condemnation. The student should be told that this is a common response and that to stop and rehearse the new skill in imagery takes a concerted effort at first.

Take a Beginner to a "Cliff"

Every time you take a run you have many opportunities to practice mental skills. Unfortunately, these opportunities are often overlooked by instructors and their students. Here is an example of a simple tactic that is educational, fun to do, and applicable to many instances. The covert point of this game is to get people relaxed enough to be able to take note of their original self-talk and prepare them for more useful coping thoughts.

Whenever you get the opportunity (for example, on a catwalk crossing), stop at the top of a double black diamond "cliff" and look over the edge. As you do, have your students do a tension check/release, and have them pay attention to their thoughts and/or images. Reassure them that they are not going to go down there, that they are just looking. Have them concentrate on what it looks like, monitoring their mental and physical tension levels. Remind them that although they do not have the skills to ski this just yet, there will come a time when they do. They can then take a moment to do another tension check/release.

This tactic will increase their familiarity with what steep and/or bumpy runs look like and with potential problems in their imagery or self-talk. Then, when they are technically ready to ski it, they will have a jump on the mental preparation. In other words, teach students to practice looking and to practice competent and calming self-statements. This is one of those little things you can do which risks nothing but allows you to give practice at taking a chance.

Make Use of Lift Time

Since at least half the time in skiing is actually spent riding the lift, continue to take advantage of this time by teaching mental skills relevant to constructive thinking. Here are two examples of things you can ask your students to work on:

1. Have the students memorize coping or countering self-statements that have been tailored for them. When you get to the appropriate situation, have them repeat the self-statement aloud and reinforce it.
2. Have them watch skiers below without evaluating, simply describing to their partner what they see. Ask their partners to monitor whether their descriptions include any negative self-statements or fear-talk such as "I could never do that," "I wonder if I look that dumb," or "That hill really looks scary."

10—Concentration

Become more sensitive to your students' levels of concentration. If you see students intently focused on what they are doing, don't interrupt. Save your comments for after they have finished their run.

If you see that they are distracted, ask them what they are aware of. Then take them through the exercises in this chapter. If they seem stuck on a particular thought or image, take them through the "station-switching" exercise until they learn that they can change focus. If their concentration is diffuse, take them through the "on" exercise of narrowed focusing. Instead of the word "on," have them focus on a simple image on the slope, the top of their ski pole, or a tree in the distance. Then have them do the same thing with a kinesthetic image, such as the sensation of their feet being pushed up as they absorb a gentle bump.

11—Metaphors: Connections Between Your Mind and Your Body

Sources for Metaphors

In one sense, every exercise in this book, and probably every exercise you give your students, is a metaphor. Exercises that employ new ways of thinking, feeling, and imaging all serve one purpose in ski performance: to connect the operating powers of the mind with the executing powers of the body. Thus the list of metaphors for skiing is infinite. You can get them from anywhere, but you have three easily available sources for them. One of them is this book. Throughout it, and especially in this chapter, we have listed the ones we like best. Some you will like and some you will not. Select the ones that work for you and your students. Tailor them as you do with other mental skills.

The second source of metaphors is *your* mind. We continue to be impressed with the creativity that instructors bring to their teaching. The only problem is that many of you are reluctant to let your minds flow when thinking of ski metaphors. One of the best ways for you to have access to the creative part of your mind is *not* to think about it. Rather, we suggest that you try to experience, with kinesthesia, mental imagery, and emotional arousal, what you are trying to teach. Put yourself in different roles: the frightened student, the self-critical student, the stubborn student, the distracted student. Then imagine what you would say or do to correct the problem. Frequently an image or metaphor will come to mind. Try it out with your next class. As is typical of metaphors, you will find that some will work and some will not. Keep the former and discard the latter.

The third source of metaphors is your students' minds. Just as you should ask them what they are thinking and feeling so you can help them overcome their present difficulties, so should you ask them what has worked for them to overcome their past problems. They will often provide you with material that you can use for other students with similar problems. And just as fear is contagious, so is creativity. Once you have introduced metaphors to your students, they will be primed to think creatively and to volunteer images and metaphors as well.

12—Falling Out of Your Mind

Instructors Never Fall?

An instructor friend of ours has a lot of fun with groups by doing a carefully planned pratfall. He uses a catwalk that lends itself beautifully to this. Just before a sharp bend in the road, he stops his group and tells them to stay to the uphill side through the turn because of the steep drop-off on the downhill side. He then goes around the bend, turns around to face the group, and slides backward over the edge, disappearing into the deep snow. The group's initial panic always turns to glee as they see him surface, covered with snow, with a giant grin on his face. Although from above the drop-off looks like a steep cliff, from up close it is merely a 2-foot drop into a small basin of soft snow. Our friend then invites anyone from the group to join him, and often someone will dive right in. It's a very good way to relieve anxiety about falling and the tension that goes with it.

Practice Falling

In this chapter we suggested that readers practice falling, first without and later with skis to desensitize themselves to their fear of falling. This exercise can double as a warm-up at the beginning of a lesson. After some initial stretching, have your class take a few standing falls. If the snow is soft, have them roll around in it until they feel like carefree kids again (a real task with many adult students). If the snow is hard-packed, have them practice falling by doing "second base slides" to spread the impact across rather than onto the hard-pack. Like most behaviors, if you demonstrate doing it with glee, they will likely follow suit.

Perfect Falls

In addition to having students practice falling with and without skis, tell them that over the course of the lesson you expect each of them to execute at least one perfect fall. A perfect fall is one that is followed by a tension check/release, an awareness review of how it occurred, a mental image that rehearses the proper action to increase the probability of recovery next time, and some positive self-statements congratulating themselves on accomplishing their assignment. Anyone who has not executed a perfect fall before the end of the lesson gets snowballed!

13—Getting Stuck on a Horrendous Hill

Coping Skills and Survival Training

Coping with a difficult situation is unpleasant for most of us. In ski instruction we are so focused on how to do things right so our students can avoid difficult situations that we often do not prepare them for those "horrendous" hills. If you have a student or class for more than two lessons, we recommend that you take them through a coping exercise. This is analogous to the strategy in Outward Bound programs in which, once adequate skills are learned, the individual has an opportunity to put them into action by coping with a difficult environment.

After you have taught your students the appropriate skills of relaxation, imagery, and constructive self-talk, as well as the necessary skiing skills, tell them that you are going to do a survival exercise. It is not the purpose of this exercise to ski well. Rather, *the purpose is to cope with and survive a difficult situation.* Have them mentally rehearse the material in this chapter so that they will be prepared. Then take them to a short run that is somewhat (but not unrealistically) over their heads and talk them through their descent. This includes physical skills such as side-slipping and wedging, as well as the mental skills included in P.R.A.Y.-ing such as tension check/releasing, relabeling, and using modeling. Once they have completed their descent, be sure to reinforce them for *coping*, not for their skiing technique. Also be sure that they reinforce themselves rather than rehearsing self-condemnation or failure imagery.

14—Helping the Minds of Your Friends

Helping the minds and bodies of your friends is what ski instruction is all about. Keep up the good work!

15—Believing and Confidence

As instructors, we are all too familiar with the picture of the glamorous ski instructor: deeply tanned face, healthy and vigorous, with attractive members of the opposite sex trailing along as they gracefully swoop through the untracked powder day after exciting day.

But we know the reality. The crowds and confusion of the Christmas rush, the scrounging for work during the January lull, the exhaustion of 21 straight days during spring break. So why do we do it? Our reasons are as varied as we are, but there is one we all share. It has to do with vicarious learning, believing and confidence, peak performances and peak experiences. As professional skiers, we know the peak experience. We also know that it is as elusive as that perfectly clean turn. But we can share those moments of peak experiences that our clients have. By providing them with new experience, by sharing their performance accomplishments, by opening up the way for growth in their self-confidence, we help them attain their breakthroughs. This in turn leads to a peak experience, *and their high rubs off on us.* And that's the bottom line.

Further Thoughts for Competitors

F or those of you who are racing or freestyle competitors, the systematic use of mental skills is a valuable tool that could provide you the winning edge. Although we have included numerous examples of competitors' use of psychological strategies throughout this book, we want to add several points. Because your goals and your commitment differ from those of most other skiers, your use of mental skills must also differ. You have set yourself apart from the average recreational skier.

Belief and Confidence

For you, the psychology of peak performance is about what you think and what you believe, and about how you blend mental skills with your skiing to form your thoughts and your beliefs. It is about how you respond to your sports environment, how you anticipate upcoming performances, and how you transform the race course into a superb challenge or the mogul field into a beautiful line.

What you think and what you believe is carried around with you. It is uniquely personal, sometimes difficult to change, and always a challenge to work with. It has evolved from your skiing accomplishments, your interpretations of the experience of others as you watch them ski, and your interpretation of your own skiing experiences.

Belief and confidence (self-efficacy) is critical. From the chapter on belief and confidence, recall Bandura's interpretation of how you are set apart from the average athlete.

"After [your] capabilities are perfected and massively practiced, perceived self-efficacy is often the difference between a good or a poor showing in athletic contests. This is because with highly perfected skills, a small lapse in effort or accuracy makes a major difference in outcome."

If you have not done so already, give a thoughtful reading to this chapter. In fact, as a competitor your reading of the book could have started with that material. Before you begin your systematic program of mental skills training, understand how belief in yourself grows through use of the specific psychological techniques set forth in the preceding chapters. After you *believe* in the importance of your efficacy expectations, then begin analyzing your skiing performance, tailoring a program and proceeding to apply it with consistency.

Tailoring

A shotgun approach to the use of mental skills is inefficient and misleading. For competitors especially, this type of approach yields poor results and decreases your faith in the effectiveness of mental skills applications to sport. If you are serious about competition, then efficiency and effectiveness are cornerstones of your training program. To that end the mental skills discussed in this book must be used *prescriptively.* That is, you and your coach must tailor your mental training program to your needs. Active awareness, the subject of chapter 4, is central to this analysis, and both you and your coach should understand it.

Your goal-setting is especially important. What aspects of your skiing do you and your coach think need work? Once specified, the two of you should review what physical and mental skills would get you there. As part of your goal-setting process, you should take into account things you can and cannot control. In this way you can avoid frustration and increased tension. Some things you can control are your arousal level, your concentration, your imagery, your choice of wax. Some things you cannot control are your competition, the course, or the weather.

As you develop awareness of your style of thinking and skiing, many general questions come to mind. Here are a few examples of questions that could be asked as you attempt to focus on a tailored mental skills training program. None should appear new to you; each is based upon material covered in preceding chapters.

1. Where are you on the performance/arousal curve during practice, low-pressure competition, and high-pressure competition?
2. How do you currently use imagery, and how is it related to your practices and competitions? What sense modalities are most powerful and seem most useful to you?
3. How good are you at negative practice and relaxation skills? At what points are they most useful in terms of your patterns of arousal?
4. What cognitive interpretations do you make when you are aroused? For example, do you label your arousal "anxiety," "precompetition excitement," or what? And which response systems are predominant when aroused: cognitive, physiological, or behavioral (motor)?
5. What motor skills must be enhanced, and are they candidates for some of the straightforward operant techniques discussed in chapter 8?
6. What is your self-talk during precompetition warm-up and during the moments before your run? During your run? Afterward? Any worst-enemy or standard-setting issues here?

Once you have narrowed your definitions of problem areas, choose the mental skills appropriate to the problem. What is "appropriate" is dictated by you *and* your coach *and* the problem. For example, there is not just one approach to centering your arousal level. Effective help might be found in relaxation training, negative practice, mental rehearsal, or in changing self-talk via relabeling. You will need to reflect on your present tactics and their effectiveness. You will especially need to rely on the perceptions of your coach. He or she likely has had more experience with planned problem-solving and with observing the maturation of athletes. Your coach will have much to contribute, especially in helping to decide which strategies you seem able to apply most consistently and which work best for you.

Consistency and Discipline

You are already an elite skier (or working toward being one) and we recognize that you presently use some of the tactics in this book. Perhaps you use some of the imagery techniques. You may or may not use relabeling and conscious modification of your self-talk. You probably have not yet thought systematically about belief and self-efficacy, since few coaches teach that material. But assuming now that you have tailored a problem analysis and written a mental skills prescription, you are ready for the difficult part. *Your major task is to be consistent in your efforts to include psychological techniques as part of your training program.*

This is no small task. As we have pointed out, it takes consistency and discipline. It may even take more discipline than your physical conditioning program, because benefits are more immediately apparent than a mental conditioning program. It takes more discipline for two other reasons.

First, in our Western culture we are not used to guiding our thoughts, feelings, and beliefs. We have never been taught to emphasize that. Instead, we tend to let our minds wander and let our thoughts guide us. Few of us were ever taught to discipline our thinking through techniques such as changing self-talk or mental imagery.

Second, there is not much peer support for quiet isolation prior to practice or competition. Teammates try to keep everybody psyched up. The banter is usually aggressive, competitive, and hot. There are not many coaches who insist that teams and individuals *establish a pattern* of mental rehearsal and make that rehearsal a critical part of practice and pre-competition warm-up.

You must establish your pattern. Various things help with this. For example, you might ask for the cooperation of others around you who would distract you from what may appear to be doing nothing. You might also create a ritual for yourself, only one part of which includes mental skills work. An example of this might be working on your equipment and associating that with certain patterns of imagery.

Be consistent, but also be flexible. There is a fine line between knowing when to continue with a particular tactic and deciding when it needs to be changed. Your coach will help with this.

Resources

Elite competitors and serious recreational skiers can benefit by taking advantage of other resources. Read widely. Some excellent ideas can be found in general books on sport psychology. We would recommend that you start with two books we cite in the references: Syer and Connolly's *Sporting Body, Sporting Mind,* and Bell's *Championship Thinking.*

Your team members are also excellent resources. Let them model efficacy for you as they prepare for competition. Let your friends give you thoughtful feedback, and if it is not as useful as you would like, teach them to become actively aware and look for information that is useful to you.

If you have access to sport psychologists, you might consider taking advantage of it. Our training enables us to do a thorough analysis of the psychological events that have an impact on athletic performance. Our training also enables us to tailor a mental skills program and assess its effectiveness on an ongoing basis. With that information, it can be altered as required by your performance, your self-report, and even by events in your life.

Finally, take advantage of your coaches and other experienced skiers. They are often veterans of more competitions than you can think about and are also more likely to talk candidly about their technical errors and mental lapses than are your fellow competitors. There is much to be learned from that. Ask about what alternatives might have worked for them at the time. You will also learn a great deal if you are willing to ask them to place their errors *and* their victories in the perspective of the psychology discussed in this book.

Learning
Mental Imagery

ortunately, learning mental imagery does not take as long as learning to ski, although it does take conscientious practice. You may be weary of hearing our reiterations about conscientious practice, but you have to admit that choosing 15 minutes each day to rehearse your mental imagery in a systematic, controlled way is not a habit most of us share!

There are many approaches to learning and rehearsing imagery. Our approach is quite straightforward: We ask you to begin with a real-life scene and to fade out the scene gradually as you learn to carry it with you in your mind. We already introduced you to this approach when we showed you how to develop awareness of your kinesthetic sense in chapter 4.

In each of the following exercises, you should be aware of where you stand initially. Are you noticing that you tend to be more visual or more kinesthetic? More observing from the outside or the inside? As you do the exercises you should expect to gain increasing control of your imagery, be able to increase its intensity, and shift your point of observation. If any of the exercises seem too elementary for you, proceed to the next. Even those among us who can create intense, continuing images, however, are not exempt from practice.

Follow these suggestions for 15 minutes and then move on to other things, picking up where you left off when you begin practicing again. Thirty minutes is not going to hurt you, but if you try that in the initial rush of enthusiasm you might burn out on the whole project. Several minutes spent each day is much better than spending all of the time in one chunk at the end of each week.

Visual Imagery

Just how visual is your visual imagery? Some people claim they can close their eyes and see movies in their mind. Others claim they never forget a face, but upon questioning they say they don't really see each face as a photograph. Instead, it is more of a visual concept. The purpose of these exercises is to increase the control you have over *your* kind of visual imagery.

Find some photographs of your family. Two current ones, along with two photos from some past event that give you pleasant memories, will get you started. First, sit back and relax as best you can. It doesn't matter if your mind is wandering; wandering was included in the original design specifications for minds! We will now begin to guide that wandering.

1.   Look at one of the older photographs under a very bright light. Look first at the whole. What is the general background? Who is in it? Reconstruct some of the memories the photo brings (these will help you to recapture visual images later). Now close your eyes briefly and relax as you try to let your mind hold the visual image. Open your eyes. Try that sequence several more times, gradually increasing the length of time your eyes are closed. Use your pleasant memories of the events in the photo and see if that helps capture the visual images. Continue to do this a dozen times or so.

2.   Now check out your imagery. Look at and "absorb" the photo again. Closing your eyes, explore what detail you can. Name several specific items in the background. Any cars? How many? Stairs in the photo? How many? Type of clothing and colors? If you are able to close your eyes and see and literally count the stairs, you don't belong in this exercise. You have a talent rare among adults that

is called "eidetic imagery." For the rest of us, the detail is difficult to recall.

3.   Begin again by using the same photograph. Be sure the light is very bright. Look at and study the details carefully. Close your eyes briefly and recreate the image. Open your eyes. Follow the same pattern, increasing the time your eyes are closed. You will need to practice this until you begin increasing the intensity of your visual image.

You are now ready to move on to the other photographs. Try to get to the point where, after some practice, you are able to look at the photograph for very brief periods and still create your image. Then, moving past the photographs, begin to do the same practice routine with real-life scenes. Suggestions include your desk, your house, the ski run in front of you, your skis, and so forth. As you gain skill, you should increasingly be able to recreate scenes that are not immediately in front of you, and then move toward continuity.

To gain skill with continuity, begin practicing while you are a passenger in a car. Use the same technique of looking, absorbing the detail of the motion (start with a familiar route) and then closing your eyes to visualize its continuation. See the scenes passing by, increasingly vivid and continuous as you practice. We suggest that you use other cues in your environment to help you out, such as the sound of the car or the wind.

Practicing mental imagery and mental rehearsal while on your skis is the point of all this, so here are some suggestions about how and where that should be done. These suggestions address your visual sense, although we realize it is difficult to separate it from your kinesthetic sense. Try the following as visually as possible:

1.   Start with your lift time. It is especially valuable and should be used as much as is reasonable. Your lift time offers many ski images, including motion, while you are in a position just to sit back and practice. Focus on a skier who is a good model, and close and open your eyes as you did in the other exercises, gradually increasing the time your eyes are closed. Listen carefully to the sound

of other skiers and use that as an aid to increase the continuity of your image. Feel the breeze in your face. While your eyes are closed, "see" the patterns of light and shadow against your eyelids as the trees next to the lift intermittently block out the sun as you move along.

2. Take the moments before you cut loose on the next section of the hill to open and close your eyes, visualizing what is ahead. See a line through the moguls, for example, and then see yourself skiing that line. You might also use some of the time to absorb the image of a good skier, and then close your eyes and finish her run for her.

Kinesthetic Imagery

We introduced the techniques to develop your kinesthetic awareness in chapter 4. The approach we suggested required you to do some movement on skis with your eyes closed, and then to blink them intermittently as the complexity of the skiing increased. Your awareness of where your body is in space and motion and your ability to compare your actual movements with what you thought you were doing is critical to enhancing your skiing performance. In trying to help you develop your kinesthetic awareness, we were also trying to help you set better goals for improving your skiing. (If you have not practiced the exercises in chapter 4 and developed some kinesthetic awareness, the material in this appendix will be of little use to you beyond some random daydreams. Please go back if necessary.)

The next step is to move from active awareness of what is currently happening as you ski to imagery of what you wish to happen in the future. It is not as great a step as it may seem.

1. Begin by focusing on one part of your body or a specific muscle group as you ski. Do this for three or four turns. Stop. Close your eyes and create a feeling image of what your muscle group was doing. Repeat several times for one muscle group (e.g., your thighs) before moving on to another. You might consider paying particular attention to the following: the soles of your feet, the bending of your knee joints, the tension in one or both hands as you grip

your pole, the location of your arms and hands relative to the rest of your body, or the pacing and depth of your breathing.

2. Do the above exercise, closing your eyes and creating the feeling image before you push off for those few turns, then compare the projected image with your real experience. You should practice this until you are able to make accurate projections of simple skiing maneuvers.

3. Observe another skier, preferably a better one, while slightly moving your limbs with him or her. That is, use body English as you are watching. Close your eyes. Continuing to use some body English, feel your movements as you create an image of yourself skiing within the skin of that other skier. (In addition to helping you develop your ability to create kinesthetic images, there are several other benefits of this type of observation, as you have learned in chapter 7.)

4. Repeat exercise 3 in the absence of body English. Create the feeling image, eyes closed, in your mind only. This is a fine use of lift time.

As you practice the exercises you should find that it becomes easier for you to project how you wish your muscles and joints to flex, where you wish your skis to be relative to the fall line, where you wish your arms and hands to be, and what posture you wish to carry. You should now shift your emphasis.

1. Each time you stop, allow a few extra moments to create a kinesthetic image of where you are heading next. Begin by concentrating on a sequence of movements in one muscle system. With continuity in mind, rehearse the next several turns you plan to make.

2. Again, each time you stop, allow those extra moments for kinesthetic mental rehearsal. In this series, however, gradually include several other movement patterns (e.g., muscles, flex patterns of joints, and breathing). This exercise should become habitual as you learn to take advantage of many idle moments for mental rehearsal.

We know it is difficult to separate visual and kinesthetic imagery as you do these exercises. That is not a major problem unless one mode is so dominant that you are unable to in-crease the intensity and control of the other. If one mode is that dominant in your imagery, we suggest you spend much more time on the simplest exercises in the applicable exer-cise series. Since skiing involves a mixture of the visual and kinesthetic senses, your mental rehearsal should ultimately be equally as balanced. Any extra time you must spend to achieve that balance in your imagery is a good investment.

Emotional Imagery

Your ability to create emotional imagery is a double-edged sword. On one hand it is the creation of fear and anger imagery that we pointed out is a major obstacle to improvement in your skiing. On the other hand, the ability to create emotional im-ages of relaxation, confidence, skiing aggressively, joy, or hav-ing fun is extremely valuable. Creating emotional imagery is generally not a problem. However, we have found that *guiding* it is more difficult.

Emotional imagery differs from kinesthetic and visual im-agery along the dimension of control. Most of us have had the experience of having our feelings run away with us. Losing your temper is a common example; even the phrase itself im-plies lack of control. Emotional imagery has more of a life of its own when unguided and is more difficult to guide through a beginning-to-end sequence than is visual or kinesthetic im-agery. Your ability to create and change emotional imagery is an important part of several techniques you will learn to use to center your arousal levels at the optimal point on your performance/arousal curve.

Guiding your emotional imagery requires a high degree of active awareness. You must be aware of which inner and outer contexts elicit a particular emotional response. For example, if you have the experience of "choking" before a race, you would have to ask questions like this: Is the audience loud or antagonistic? Has this type of course been a problem before? Am I thinking thoughts that are antagonistic (being my own worst enemy)? Have I watched a number of racers blow out of the course at some problem gate?

We suggest you use an audiotape to help you create emotional imagery and then learn to guide it. To make an audiotape, first choose three or four situations that are typically quite arousing to you. You may be standing at the starting gate as you hear over the public address system that the racer on the course has just blown out; or you may be standing on top of a steep bump run, or getting ready to push off into a spectacular expanse of untracked powder. You should then become aware of which characteristics in each scene arouse you. Examples include what you are saying to yourself, whether you imagine you may fall at the same gate, or the anticipation of powder billowing around you.

The audiotaped scenes should be about 5 minutes long, describing in detail the arousing characteristics you have just identified. You may have to repeat several of those characteristics but that is okay. Move slowly, guiding your imagery through increasing levels of arousal.

Listen to the tape frequently enough to establish that you can create and guide your imagery in those specific scenes, and then set them aside until you wish to improve your skiing by centering the arousal you are feeling. A note of caution: If you continue listening to the negative scenarios without doing anything about your emotions, you might as well be having the same negative experiences on the mountain.

Integrated Imagery

Your imagination of skiing should ultimately be multidimensional. Visual, kinesthetic, and emotional experiences are wrapped together in a fun and rewarding package. The more you ski, and the more you use imagery as you are skiing, the easier it will become to tie all of these dimensions together both on the mountain and off. On the other hand, to ask you to create integrated images of skiing without experience on the mountain would be unrealistic. This leads us to the best assignment of all: Go gather experience on the mountain! As you do, you will find that peak experiences are more frequently created, and you will find it easier to recreate them in joyful and integrated imagery.

References

General Readings

Abraham, H. (1983). *Skiing right*. New York: Harper & Row.

Bell, K.F. (1983). *Championship thinking: The athlete's guide to winning performance in all sports*. Englewood Cliffs, NJ: Prentice-Hall.

Benson, H., & Proctor, W. (1984). *Beyond the relaxation response*. New York: Times Books.

Cousins, N. (1979). *Anatomy of an illness as perceived by the patient: Reflections on healing and regeneration*. New York: W.W. Norton.

Gallwey, T. (1977). *Inner tennis*. New York: Random House.

Gallwey, T., & Kriegel, B. (1977). *Inner skiing*. New York: Random House.

Garfield, C., & Bennett, H.Z. (1984). *Peak performance: Mental training techniques of the world's greatest athletes*. Los Angeles: Jeremy P. Tarcher, Inc.

Harris, D.V., & Harris, B.L. (1984). *The athlete's guide to sports psychology: Mental skills for physical people*. New York: Leisure Press.

Hendricks, G., & Carlson, J. (1982). *The centered athlete: A conditioning program for your mind.* Englewood Cliffs, NJ: Prentice-Hall.

Jerome, J. (1982). *The sweet spot in time.* New York: Avon.

Kappas, J.G. (1984). *Self-hypnosis: The key to athletic success.* Englewood Cliffs, NJ: Prentice-Hall.

Kauss, D.R. (1980). *Peak performance.* Englewood Cliffs, NJ: Prentice-Hall.

Klavora, P., & Daniel, J.V. (1978). *Coach, athlete, and the sport psychologist.* Champaign, IL: Human Kinetics.

Lazarus, A. (1984). *In the mind's eye: The power of imagery for personal enrichment.* New York: Guilford Press.

Leonard, G. (1975). *The ultimate athlete.* New York: Viking Press.

Loehr, J.E. (1982). *Athletic excellence: Mental toughness training for sports.* Denver: Forum Publ. Co.

Loudis, L.A., & Lobitz, W.C. (1977). *Skiing from the head down: A psychological approach.* Philadelphia: Lippincott.

McCluggage, D. (1973). *The centered skier.* New York: Bantam Books.

Nideffer, R.M. (1976). *The inner athlete: Mind plus muscle for winning.* New York: Thomas Crowell.

Orlick, T. (1980). *In pursuit of excellence.* Champaign, IL: Human Kinetics.

Pelletier, K. (1977). *Mind as healer, mind as slayer.* New York: Dell Publ.

Ryan, F. (1981). *Sports and psychology.* Englewood Cliffs, NJ: Prentice-Hall.

Suinn, R. (Ed.).(1980). *Psychology in sports: Methods and applications.* Minneapolis: Burgess.

Syer, J., & Connolly, C. (1984). *Sporting body, sporting mind: An athlete's guide to mental training.* New York: Cambridge University Press.

Tutko, T., & Tosi, U. (1976). *Sports psyching: Playing your best game all of the time.* Los Angeles: Jeremy P. Tarcher, Inc.

Technical References

Bandura, A. (1977). Toward a unifying theory of behavioral change. *Psychological Review,* **84**, 191-215.

Bandura, A. (1982). Self-efficacy mechanism in human agency. *American Psychologist,* **37**, 122-147.

Bandura, A. (1984). Recycling misconceptions of perceived self-efficacy. *Cognitive Therapy and Research,* **8**, 231-255.

Lee, C. (1982). Self-efficacy as a predictor of performance in competitive gymnastics. *Journal of Sport Psychology,* **4**, 405-409.

Mahoney, M.J. (1979). Cognitive skills and athletic performance. In P.C. Kendall & S.C. Hollon (Eds.), *Cognitive behavioral interventions: Theory, research and procedures.* New York: Academic Press.

Morgan, W.P., Horstman, D.H., Cymerman, A., & Stokes, J. (1983). Facilitation of physical performance by means of a cognitive strategy. *Cognitive Therapy and Research,* **7**, 251-264.

Ornstein, R.E. (1971). *The psychology of consciousness.* San Francisco: W.H. Freeman.

Seltz, D.L. & Landers, D.M. (1983). The effects of mental practice on motor skill learning and performance: A meta-analysis. *Journal of Sport Psychology,* **5**, 25-57.

Sperry. R.W. (1968). Hemisphere deconnection and unity in conscious awareness. *American Psychologist,* **23**, 723-733.

Suinn, R.M. (1972). Removing emotional obstacles to learning and performance by visuo-motor behavior rehearsal. *Behavior Therapy,* **3**, 308-310.

Suinn, R.M. (1972). Behavior rehearsal training for ski racers. *Behavior Therapy,* **3**, 519-520.

Suinn, R.M. (1977). Behavioral methods at the winter Olympic Games. *Behavior Therapy,* **8**, 283-294.

Weinberg, R.S., Gould, D., & Jackson, A. (1979). Expectations and performance: An empirical test of Bandura's self-efficacy theory. *Journal of Sport Psychology,* **1**, 320-331.

Weinberg, R.S., Yukelson, D., & Jackson, A. (1980). Effect of public and private efficacy expectations on competitive performance. *Journal of Sport Psychology,* **2**, 340-349.

Woolfolk, R.L., Parrish, M.W., & Murphy, S.M. (1985). The effects of positive and negative imagery on motor skill performance. *Cognitive Therapy and Research,* **9**(3), 335-341.